THIS WE CAN SAY

TALKING HONESTLY ABOUT SEX

NINE FRIENDS PRESS

READING • 1995

Designed and typeset
by Jeremy Greenwood
Woodbridge

Printed by
Warwick Printing Company Limited
Theatre Street, Warwick CV34 4DR

Published by
Nine Friends Press
PO Box 2165, Reading RG6 7YZ

ISBN 0 9525535 0 3

CONTENTS

PREFACE

No group of people brought together as we were could hope to be representative of the Religious Society of Friends. We are all white and middle class: when we began our ages ranged from late 20s to about 60. The ways in which we earn our living also are very representative of Quakers – we work in education and the caring professions. Our experience includes a variety of life-styles and commitments: bisexual, gay, heterosexual and lesbian, some living with partners, some singly. One of us is divorced and another separated from a partner. We owe a great debt of gratitude to our partners for supporting us during the five years of the group's existence, for tolerating our absences and for living with the difficult knowledge that we were discussing intimate details of our lives with others.

The middle years of the group's life were overshadowed by the illness of Gordon Macphail and Loraine Brown and the death of Gordon at the tragically early age of 35 years. Loraine's illness prevented her from attending the last two years of meetings but she remained in touch with the group and continued to write for us. From our first meeting Gordon was completely open with us about his HIV positive status. He knew and we knew that his time with us was limited, but he gave unstintingly of his energy and commitment while he could and by his presence and his writings he was an inspiration to us. We who remain gratefully dedicate this book to his memory.

David Blamires — Christine Knott
Loraine Brown — Neil Pickering
June Ellis — Elisabeth Salisbury
Colin Hunter — Chris Skidmore
Zoe White

INTRODUCTION

In 1988 a small group of Quakers met to consider rewriting, or revising, the 1963 book *Towards a Quaker view of sex* which was out of date, though it was still selling well. What had been widely regarded as a pioneering work on sexual ethics was now seen as an historical document rather than a contribution to current thought. The original authors felt the need to inform as well as to make ethical judgements; legal, biological, sociological and psychological matters were discussed in learned detail. While this was appropriate in the early 1960s, these matters should now perhaps be approached in a different spirit.

The Literature Committee of Quaker Home Service had recognised that times had changed, and had asked our group to look again at issues of sex and sexuality and to see whether it was possible to produce a *Towards a Quaker view of sex* for our times. The late 1980s was the age of AIDS, the moral majority and the Paedophile Information Exchange, an age looking back from a distance of a quarter of a century on the paperback publication of *Lady Chatterley's lover*, and the 'permissive' sixties. That was the context of our first meeting, and naturally the ten of us were rather nervous.

There were several kinds of book that we might have considered trying to write, and each of them might have had its place. We might have tried to write a definitive Quaker statement on sexuality. We might have written a book intended to update *Towards a Quaker view of sex* or to present a new and radical paradigm for relationships among human beings and between human beings and God. Any of these might have been worth doing, but none of them is what we felt led to do when we first met, or what we have actually done. In that sense we have not fulfilled the hopes that Literature Committee had for us. This book is therefore an independent publication and in no sense an official Quaker statement.

We took it that we should try to respond as honestly as possible to the question, 'What canst thou say?' And perhaps we all had in mind the story of Jesus and the woman taken in adultery, that we should beware of a certain kind of judgement. We tried not to let our own opinions get in the way of listening to each other or reading what we had written. Notwithstanding this spirit of openness, this is not a book which proclaims that there are no rules. None of us as individuals believes that. Neither is it a book which proclaims that there is one way to be, or one way to live. It does not attempt to undermine sexual guilt or the sense of failure which is a reality for some – some of us too. It does not reject the possibilities of remaking ourselves, of change, of growth, which are realities for others – some of us too. It does not proclaim that sex and spirituality are necessarily conjoined – though for some of us that is the case, and for others the hope.

We want to get away from the idea of hierarchies of sexual experience. Even books which purport to be tolerant nevertheless give the impression that it's best to be a heterosexual parent with 2.4 children living in a stable relationship in which the participants have sex x times a week. We want people to know that it's acceptable to be celibate, childless, straight, gay, lesbian, bisexual: that none of these conditions is better than another.

We want to get across the idea that there isn't a right or a wrong way to 'do sex', as long as the relationship is one in which the lovers respect and care for each other. Many of us have spent so much of our lives feeling inadequate because, according to the books, we didn't 'do it' properly. We want the shy, lonely and frightened (particularly the young, but you can be shy, lonely and frightened at 50 as well as 15) to read our book and feel a sense of relief that they are not alone. Many sex books made us feel completely inadequate. Out there were all these people having this fantastic sex life, imaginative, multi-orgasmic and fulfilling – and we were excluded from this club.

We want to help people give up any thought that there are experts who will tell you how to do it properly – pray, love, even cook. All we can say is, 'This is how it was for us at a certain time but it's bound to be different for you'.

We do not know which parts of our book will speak to which readers. We do not know in what light we will be seen, having said what we have said here. So, this is our final act of faith as a group: though each piece was written by one person only among the ten of us, we all own everything that is said here and have joined together to publish what we have written.

We shall always be grateful to the Literature Committee of Quaker Home Service for asking us to meet and funding our meetings. Though they did not finally feel able to publish this book, they provided us with the spur to begin our task and bore with us prayerfully through much of its gestation. Our acts of faith, in trusting to the process as it revealed itself through our meetings and, now, in setting this book before you, are mirrored by the acts of faith which our loved ones, from both within and outside the Society of Friends, have made in supporting us and what we have done. Our thanks go out to our partners, husbands, wives, close friends, children and parents; they appear in this book anonymously and unavoidably. No one but us, however, is responsible for what is written here.

REFLECTIONS

Our Quaker tradition and its consequences

> 'Are there not different states, different degrees, different growths, different places...'
>
> Isaac Penington, 1667

> 'One of life's hardest lessons is that there is no justification for expecting that our neighbour is to traverse precisely the same path as we ourselves have followed.'
>
> William Littleboy, 1916

> '... our vision of the truth has to be big enough to include other people's truth as well as our own.'
>
> Beth Allen, 1984

These statements express something central about the way we have sought to work and also about the way in which we hope that this book will be received.

We have been aware of an expectation on the part of some Friends that we would provide a statement of the Quaker approach to sexuality, and perhaps some prescriptions about how Quakers ought to behave sexually. This could not be that kind of book, because Quakers are wary of that kind of authority.

As Quakers we feel ourselves to be seekers and, in our task, have tried to be open to the spirit and to record only that which springs from our living experience. We are not presenting a finished truth. As Harold Loukes has written, in a different context, 'our point of departure is not a mighty proclamation of Truth, but a humble invitation to sit down together and share what we have found...'* Paradox and tension have abounded as we have, in our human way, searched for

* Harold Loukes, *God speaking through us,* in Maurice Creasey and Harold Loukes, *The next 50 years,* 1956, p 58, quoted in *Quaker faith and practice,* 1995, ¶28.08.

answers and found yet more questions. And this is part of our Quaker way, that everything can be questioned in trying to live our lives according to the spirit.

More than three hundred years ago, George Fox went beyond the limitations of his time and proclaimed true religion as a living response to that which is to be found within each of us. In his own life he struggled and found no easy answers but instead was engaged in exploring what it is to be fully human, discovering spirituality as grounded in his own experience, rather than in traditional religious teachings. And, of course, this resulted in a radical change in the way he saw the world, in the way he acted. From this inwardness stemmed an awareness of the oneness of all people and the oneness of life.

The vision he articulated lives on. For Quakers the whole of life is sacred, to be lived in the Spirit. We cannot separate our religion from our life if it is to be authentic, and so we cannot separate our sexual experiences from our religious experiences. We have found again and again that in exploring our sexuality we have also been discovering our spirituality for, in the heights and depths of our experience, they are one. And spirituality, like sexuality, is about darkness as well as light.

Perhaps initially some of us felt we would be able to articulate some kind of Quaker viewpoint but in our worship and in our work together we have become clear that just as we don't have an agreed set of rules requiring religious obedience so we cannot have a set of such rules to follow in our sexual lives. That would be a denial, at the deepest level, of our Quakerism. Believing this, we have found ourselves able to write only from our living experience, knowing that what we write is both partial and provisional but, at the same time, knowing our personal visions to have been both broadened and deepened as they have been tested out within our Quaker discipline.

George Trevelyan* wrote of the Quakers that, in essence, they believed 'that Christian qualities matter much more than Christian dogma'. It is from this position that we are writing, but we did not find that this enabled us to avoid hard decisions. In some ways it is easier to have moral certainties according to which to try to lead our lives. We fail, of course, but we know where we are. But should we judge others by these standards? We shall find it hard to treat them in the same way. We may be in danger of cutting ourselves off from that

* George Trevelyan, *English social history*, Longmans, 1944, p 267.

of God within them. Absolute, unalterable rules do not take account of the sheer untidiness of life and, moreover, can conflict with Jesus' command to love, which places people above rules. Isaac Penington is very perceptive here:

> Let him that stands take heed lest he fall; and mourn over and wait for the restoring of him that is fallen. That which is so apt to be offended, is the same as that which falls. O! do not reason in the high-mindedness, against any that turn aside from thy pure Guide; but fear, lest the unbelieving and fleshly-wise part get up in thee also. O know the weakness of the creature in the withdrawings of the life; and the strength of the enemy in that hour, and the free grace and mercy which alone can preserve; and thou wilt rather wonder that any stand, than that some fall.*

Sexuality itself is a gift of God. We acknowledge and celebrate the glory of sexuality: we must not forget the dark side. The openness to and acceptance of the other that can be at the heart of sexual relationships mean that rejection and damage can be great when we fail. When we are close to meeting that of God in others, the opportunity for sin may not be far away. However, the right exercise of our sexuality has various expressions. We need to accept this variety as part of the diversity of creation. But we also need to recognise that, like all God's gifts, our sexuality can be misused. The fact that everything happens does not mean that anything goes.

This does not mean we are saying it does not matter what we do. We are not advocating some kind of anarchic romantic position. Rather, we affirm that all life is one and that in seeking to live our lives we strive to live experimentally in the same spirit that guided George Fox. Quakerism is not an easy option: our faith does not provide us with any kind of feather-bedding. We are required to walk hand in hand with uncertainty (which doesn't, paradoxically, preclude a sureness of a different sort).

Christian tradition has for long periods been identified with a narrowly prescriptive, judgemental theology which has continually attempted to place restrictions on sexual relationships and sexual expression. We have to accept our part in this Christian tradition and realise that Christianity's unwillingness, over long periods of its history,

* Isaac Penington from an undated letter to an unnamed correspondent in *A month with Isaac Penington*, edited by Beatrice Saxon Snell, Quaker Home Service, 1966.

to regard sexuality with delight has led to the suppression of much valuable experience. And we need to look again at these restrictions, at the insistence on marriage as the only appropriate context for sexual relationships, at our ideas of some forms of sexual activity as perverse, perhaps even at our ideas of marriage itself. We must subject them continually to the searching gaze of the Inward Light and ask whether they are still serviceable. One of us has written:

> If you find that your experience is contained, fully and happily, within the traditional forms, then you are lucky. But it is not everyone's experience, despite the fact that marriage has been marketed as though it were the optimum solution for everybody except self-chosen celibates. The realities of sexual experience are like mercury, not at all easy to handle, bright and unexpectedly fluid. Sexual experience consists of disappointments and embarrassments as well as bliss and happy discoveries.

Quakers, who seek to be open to the light from whatever quarter it may arise, need to be open to the possibility of change and of new insights, uncomfortable though they may be. Sometimes, in seeking to avoid conflict, we paper over the cracks and what is hidden can fester and destroy the energy of a group or meeting, failing to recognise the creative value of difference, and the new life that can come from tension. It is important to note the human tendency in the face of difference and uncertainty to retreat into 'unthinking', into dogmatism and unexamined opinions.

We are saying there are no easy answers; we are certainly saying we have no easy answers to lay before you. We are not, however, saying we can never judge behaviour. We know shame and guilt in our own lives and can say, 'I know that to have been wrong', and daily we meet temptation. But we also know that things that seemed wrong, or bad, have had consequences that we could not have imagined, that have been positive and creative. It may often be in failure that we come closer to God and even to being a vehicle of God for others. In this way our sexual relationships can help to deepen our spiritual journey. Our vulnerability and closeness to failure are part of the lesson as also is the experience of forgiveness. So we feel a profound humility, and have to acknowledge a great deal of 'not knowingness' in the face of life's mysteries.

In affirming that people are more important than rules, we are not denying that we have responsibilities. All our actions have consequences that must be thought about, perhaps prayed about, especially where children are concerned. Finding discernment may not be easy because we do not necessarily know what consequences will ensue. For some, a dark and difficult experience – which feels like death – may be the beginning of a birth. And that dark and difficult experience may be to stay in a relationship; or to leave it; or to be left. When we are tempted to judge other people it is important to remember how impossible it is ever to know what goes on inside from the outside of a relationship.

If we are to ask, in line with our Quaker tradition, 'and what canst thou say?' we are not also condemning people to a totally individual, privatised existence. As part of a religious community we are not islands but members one of another. We therefore have a responsibility not only to hold up our own behaviour to the Inward Light but to challenge others to do likewise. We need to establish an atmosphere of trust and acceptance among us where loving rebuke is possible and where we may watch over each other in a spirit of wisdom and compassion. Let us remember, when we seek for discernment in these difficult, painful, joyous areas of our lives, that we have a Quaker heritage which will not provide us with the answers but which will provide us with a way of seeking clearness, guided always by John Woolman's description of love as 'the first motion'.

The group's process

As we met for our first session, we knew rather little about one another, and some of us were meeting for the first time. We were used to Quaker committees and – having allowed our names to go forward – ready to do the work. At the same time, we were cautious and uncertain of what the task was and whether, indeed, there was a task.

Something powerful was catalysed in us in that first meeting. We opened ourselves up to sexuality, and felt its awesome power. This left us with a sense that we were committing ourselves to a journey that would be costly and that could play havoc with our tidy boundaries. For some, there was a feeling of panic (and maybe the god Pan is an important figure; a god, yes, but a god with a cloven hoof and one whose music sent ripples of fear vibrating through the undergrowth). One member of the group probably expressed what we were all feeling, and circulated a letter afterwards voicing fear and doubts about continuing. But we all went on together.

As our meetings continued, we went beyond Quaker grey, beyond our serviceable personae and discovered (or had discovered for us, for we often felt at the mercy of compelling forces) vast hinterlands with interweaving themes, found out things about ourselves that we had not known or perhaps had needed to forget.

The process we used throughout, both for our meetings and for writing, reflects the traditional Quaker theology of speaking in our own voices, from our own experience; attending to 'that of God' in others and not judging in our hearts. In practice, these basic ideas expressed themselves in creative listening on themes which were agreed upon in advance of each meeting. As well as listening, we sometimes discussed, and even argued. Occasionally, we laboured with one another over complex and highly charged moral issues, but we did not focus primarily here. Rather, the process we lived was one of holding together many disparate and varied life experiences, and we also found that we, as a group, were held and bound together, in and through the sharing of them.

Yet we are a varied group with diverse backgrounds and experience; individuals amongst us are struggling in different ways with the meanings of spiritual life for themselves. Indeed, it would be true to say that each of us is sceptical, in some degree, about the intellectual and spiritual positions which others of us hold. Each one of us has, at different times, felt that we were the odd one out, the one-off that prevented the others from reaching a desired unity.

At our afternoon and weekend meetings we ate together, and shared some basic chores. We often laughed. Sometimes one of us would cry as he or she spoke. Despite our apparent differences, we became close.

Most of what we said in our meetings is not recorded except in the briefest of notes. But that is as it should be, we feel. Most of the ministry we hear in Meeting for Worship each Sunday is 'unrecorded' in the same way; but there is no necessary sense of loss – though from time to time we all wished that we had got down in some form what some one of us had shared. But, even if we had taped it all, the spoken word does not always do well written down. The following extracts – exceptionally noted down at a session by one of us – reveal something of our process as we talked of our feelings about the exercise of the group and how it changed us:

❖

I found the listening very moving and so much that was unexpected. When there was patience and love in the group to listen 'from where it came' I felt a powerful sense of solidarity. I found that honesty and vulnerability in others elicited a deep sympathy in me. With regard to telling things to the group it took a long time to say certain sorts of things, a long time appropriately and willingly to feel as if they could be said, because sexuality is a tangled subject.

❖

I've changed tremendously since the beginning of the group. I thought you were all virtuous good Quakers and I was the odd-ball. I've found we are either all virtuous or all odd-balls. It's amazing how wrong you can be when you make assumptions. I really think telling my story is essential, and yet I've never had a chance to do it. I've held onto things either because I was ashamed or felt it wasn't important.

❖

As the life of the group has progressed I have been able to share feelings that previously I would have kept hidden. During the first meetings I tended to intellectualise and argue. Gradually I listened more – and it was the listening that changed me. Through the listening I was able to accept individuals in the group because they were making themselves vulnerable and opening up part of their deeper selves. This in turn gave me the space and permission to begin to open up myself in an atmosphere of acceptance, at first awkwardly and tentatively, and not without some hurt and bruising. This didn't mean I necessarily agreed with all the others' views, opinions and beliefs. There are differences that have not been resolved. But in being accepted and valued by the group, and accepting them for who they were, I found that I could more easily accept myself.

❖

The most difficult thing for me has been writing my own story. I've shared here more than anywhere else. We are all different, yet a unity gradually came out of that diversity. I've found that however unsympathetic a view I have of someone, if I open out and trust, then the unity is there; the response is there; the learning is there.

❖

I share the importance of the sense of trust. I too have said things I haven't said to anyone else, and I think telling our own stories has been important. I rarely see other members of the group in between meetings. There are ways in which I feel that the ME who comes to our meetings is different to the ME in the rest of my life. I wonder which is the real me?

❖

I've felt close in these experiences and connected in a deep way with something that is both unique and universal. Listening has been incredibly real, important and moving. When it comes to telling, there are different feelings around. I've felt great difficulties in sharing. I've felt an outsider and this has been a pattern in my life. I've felt I haven't been able to contribute anything valuable, though it was liberating when I did write things down.

It wasn't so much what was said that surprised me – though the variety of experience has been enormous for such a small group, I wonder if this would be the same for every mixed group of ten people? – but that such intimate and revealing things were said at all. I'm naturally reticent on what to me are important personal matters but, bit by bit, being in the group has allowed me to 'come out'.

It's hard to live with failure. There's nothing you can do about it. There's this need I have to talk and finish unfinished business. I can't bear the unfinishedness of it. I've never really talked about it. I don't feel I have a right to be heard – my story isn't worth hearing. I wonder how many other people think that?

I've also felt the gift and relief of hearing others' stories. The fact of our differences has not been significant, it's the honesty and humanness that has been important, and being able to locate and connect these feelings in myself. It's good to be released from isolation, to release my experience and put it in a larger human arena of experience and consciousness. We have become friends and grown together as a group.

❖

From an early stage we started writing pieces as a separate exercise. Sometimes we wrote on subjects we had all agreed to attempt to write about, sometimes on subjects or events and feelings we individually wished to write about. It was from these pieces of written material that we selected the contents of this book.

You may wonder what the relationship between the sharing in creative listening at our meetings and the writing at home might be. The main link was the group itself. We knew, when we wrote, who we were writing for, we knew in what spirit our pieces would be read, and in what way the writer would be affirmed and accepted by the others.

There was sometimes a confessional quality about our sharing and we found that the more we risked being revealed – especially in our guilt or shame, or in our feelings of inferiority or failure – the more we discovered ourselves to be at one with each other. Though the details of our experience were very different, we were each able to see ourselves reflected in the honest self-revelation of others. It was a process which began to unlock the truth within each one of us and enabled us to begin to accept the ambiguity, confusion and mess, as well as the joys and challenges of our lives. In this way, we were knit together and revealed to each other in our one common experience – that of being human.

Perhaps one of the greatest challenges of the process was development of the willingness to let go of our preconceived notions of rightness, and simply be present to ourselves, and to each other in an open-hearted way. This was difficult because, of course, such radically open presence to each other is not merely passive or neutral; once begun, the process reveals deeper levels of risk, inviting us to allow ourselves to be touched and transformed by the stories of other lives and by the Spirit which lives and moves within and among us.

It was not always easy to listen without judgement, especially when we heard experience which shocked or which seemed incomprehensible, politically incorrect or 'unquakerly'. Nevertheless, we remained faithful to the process, believing that true peace and justice (in matters sexual, as in all other aspects of our lives) can only be brought about via a restoration of our sense of belonging to a common human condition which is ultimately only revealed and redeemed through a patient, attentive love which knows no bounds.

LIVING FULLY

The passions of our lives cause us often to be mixed up, unclear and out of our depth. Not only is this true of our own individual experience, it has also been true of our process as a group.

As we have told our stories, we have found over and over that we cannot separate the evil and the good in our lives – they are intertwined; and, paradoxically, good can come from evil and evil can be brought about by good. We have held experiences of intimacy and desire alongside those of alienation and degradation; communion alongside confusion and despair. In the same way, the spiritual and the sexual have been interwoven. Nor has it been possible to concentrate on sexuality alone, for we have found it to irradiate every part of our lives.

We are at pains to assert that sexual experience, which often tends to be associated only with active genital behaviour, is in fact something much wider and more mysterious, with an immense potential for joy and celebration and for despair and agony. We know the heights and the depths in our sexuality (as in our spirituality). At a deep level they may be seen to share the same source and impulsion: union with another; union with God.

And just as, as Quakers, we do not distinguish the sacred from the secular and every day is a holy day, so all life is permeated by our sexuality from birth till death. This goes far beyond physical response, which is only part of a much more overarching human reality. It influences our feelings about ourselves and our relations with others, enlivening and enriching our life, whether or not we are actively engaged in a sexual relationship.

For us, living fully is about saying 'yes' to life's experiences, about acknowledging the parts of ourselves that we normally keep hidden, and trusting that there can be meaning in the darkest of experiences. As we more and more find room within ourselves to acknowledge our capacity for darkness (as, indeed, George Fox did) then the nearer we come to being as God intended and the less we need to lay our darkness on other people. Living fully is about opening ourselves to ambiguity and mystery, about suspending judgement.

Living fully is also about saying 'yes' to our childhood experiences and these were often the basis of our sharing. Vivid memories jostled together in the small room where we met. Again and again we were transported to earlier worlds and connected in powerful ways with the children we once were. We shared some of the rapture of childhood, the experience of merging without fear; we were touched by the pain and loss that can fill a child's universe; we were often moved to tears and affected by another's distress; we were drawn close and became part of one another's lives. The experiences we relived had indelibly marked the persons we had become, and they were still alive within us.

Our sexuality, such a significant part of who we are, is inevitably bound up with these early experiences, especially with our parents. But whatever the reality of our childhoods, what we have been powerfully aware of has been the creative power of the present moment; of how the circumstances of our early lives can be changed by the way in which we come to view them. As Tom Robbins says, 'It's never too late to have a happy childhood.'

The metaphor of ourselves as children is fertile. Many of our truest moments were when we were in touch with this archetypal child that lives in us all and incorporates both suffering and joy, the human and the divine. In our group there was a kind of redemption and celebration of this inner child as we shared jokes and played with ideas and possibilities, were content, at times, simply to be rather than to strive. And in the openness and fun we felt that we reached the part of ourselves that is closest to God.

Of course, we were and are adults seeking to work in the Light; and for those of us who are parents there is a tremendous sense of joy in our children and at how much we have learnt from them. But just as we are all symbolically children, so we are also symbolically parents, and can choose to nurture and care for our inner child.

To live fully is not to be reduced to any simple formula. In our own experiences we have been aware of the diversity, the paradox and the sheer mess that is life.

For some, life-long partnerships have not featured in our lives and this has brought fresh opportunities as well as losses. We acknowledge that the decision to opt for celibacy can be a passionate redefinition of one's sexuality. Some of our most important relationships have been short-term. Some of our failed relationships are, with all the heartache, not to be regretted. We know that we have caused pain to others, and that this continues. But if we are to live fully, we must risk and sometimes this means failure.

We struggle with uncertainty, discomfort and paradox, and whilst exulting in the passion and delight of falling in love yet know the importance of a commitment that may be hard and costly but through which providence moves and great things become possible.

We have experienced sadness and loss. There have been dark and difficult times for each one of us and yet there has been a striving towards living fully and in our relations together we have risked and been accepted. There has been conflict. There has been growth.

The intimacy we have known, in which we have been able to be ourselves, to let ourselves be known by others and to be comfortable with this, has perhaps been the most important part of our work together. It has been a kind of grace and truly transformational.

The pieces that follow are extracts from longer pieces of writing by members of the group. Each is a personal expression of experience. They have been grouped loosely under five headings.

Becoming ourselves

Many of the extracts in this section return to childhood in search of understanding present difficulties, challenges and patterns of behaviour. Sometimes we have to fight the dragons of our childhood in order to move further into the possibilities of creative relationships.

Adolescence is also a significant time in our lives. Young people begin to question the views of their parents and other adults and often find them lacking. There may be conflicts and tensions about how young people should live.

But into adulthood the shadow stalks us. Those potential traits within us that have been sublimated, or have not had the opportunity to be experienced, may make themselves known in uncomfortable or even frightening ways. These aspects too are included here for they are part of our wholeness.

I grew up in tremendous ignorance of sexual matters and even now as a middle-aged woman I realise that my knowledge is still patchy. I learnt very little from my mother and nothing at all from my father. At high school there was one formal lesson on reproduction in rabbits. Informally we girls chatted a lot and even checked out each other's developing bodies but still ignorance prevailed. I remember my two elder sisters laughing when I tried to find out about things from my mother. I had no idea that what I had picked up on the beach while on a church youth club holiday was a condom. The boys in the gang told my best friend to talk to me. I did not know how babies were born until I was seventeen when my eldest sister had her first baby. My mother told me that she had to have stitches. I thought all mothers had to have stitches because all babies were born by operation. It seems so silly now but in fact such ignorance is dangerous. I suppose I learnt a lot from magazines, books and dictionaries and also the leaflet that came with the first box of tampons. I also learnt a lot from kindly boyfriends and later my husband. What if they had been unkind?

❖

As far as I can remember, my mother answered my questions about sex fairly straightforwardly before I reached puberty. I don't remember my father being much, if at all, involved in this process, but as I was an omnivorous reader I think most of my information came from the problem pages of women's magazines, and my questions arose from things that I didn't understand in my reading. I don't think I learnt anything directly from my parents about the sexual changes that come with puberty, but my memory is cloudy.

❖

I read somewhere that 'memory' and 'mourning' have a common root. If so then it is apposite because in my memories I have a strong sense of lost possibilities. So much of what I remember is covert, oblique, uneasy and with little joy.

As a child, sex – in our house – was a 'no-go' area; never openly acknowledged. It was as if it did not exist.

I don't think I was given any inkling of periods, though I knew, through talking at school that something would happen. When my periods did start, my mother took me on one side (and that phrase sounds right) and, in hushed tones, explained about 'being unwell'; that it would happen once a month; that I was a woman now. She stressed that, at all costs, this monthly happening had to be kept from 'the men' (my father and brothers).

Sanitary towels were an unknown refinement in my home and the flow was stemmed by 'cloths'. They were washed and used over and over again. They were bulky and, because there was a need to wear them for as long as possible to keep down on washing, they often chafed painfully. In summer, it was a particular problem, they were malodorous and sometimes the flesh at the top of my legs was broken so that walking was difficult. Going to university was a tremendous liberation and not least in that it freed me to be able to buy sanitary towels.

❖

My personal background taught me that the spontaneous expression of emotions, whether of joy, love, anger or grief, was wrong. This wasn't voiced explicitly, no one said, 'Thou shalt not cry, wail, rant, rave, dance, jump about or throw the dishes.' I learnt this lesson by example. I simply never saw emotion happen.

I saw other children crying at school, but I knew that this was 'childish' behaviour. My school rewarded 'mature', 'responsible' behaviour, not shouting, swearing or fighting. Of course, it's not a bad thing to learn that swearing and fighting are not the most effective way of settling a dispute, but the settling of disputes was not what was being taught here. What I learned was that being a mature, responsible adult meant being in control of your emotions. It never dawned on me that much 'adult' behaviour I saw on TV (Westerns, for example) was far from being 'controlled'. I just went on assuming that it must be 'responsible' because it was 'adult'.

Emotions existed in our family, but they were more like an undercurrent of moods and withdrawals which seeped out just below the surface. When you looked at the surface everything was calm and 'happy'; when you felt underneath, there were undercurrents and you had to try to read and respond to these as best you could. In order to deal with this, I withdrew, I didn't respond to anything, I learned how to be 'nice'.

❖

I was brought up in a very loving family. I never knew my parents have a serious misunderstanding with each other or quarrel. My father would give my mother an affectionate kiss when he set off to work in the morning and when he returned. As a small child I would creep into my parents' bed in the morning, so my father would kiss me too and I remember his stubbly chin. My father was 38 when I was born, so he was on the brink of middle age. My mother was five years younger.

Dad was an undemonstrative, gentle sort of person. It may be significant that I did not come out as gay until after my father's death, but retrospectively I am sorry that I was not ready to talk to my father about it. I think that he would have been supportive about it, as my mother always was. She had certain difficulties at first, since she had to come to terms with it by herself, but she did not let me know that she had been upset until quite a long time afterwards.

My mother was a sociable, outgoing kind of person. She made friends easily and was generous in hospitality, an excellent cook and knitter. She and her three sisters all kept spotless houses. I can't imagine anyone not liking either of my parents. Yet there were a few things that happened in my childhood which caused me to feel unsure and mistrustful of her. On one occasion she read my diary when I was in my early teens, and what she read disturbed her. It was to do with nudity out of doors, and I was more or less forced to promise I wouldn't do it again. I later felt that this promise was extracted under duress and was thus invalid. The result of this discovery of my mother's was that I ceased to write any further entries of this sort in my diary and that I realised that such quasi-sexual and sexual matters were liable to upset her. It wasn't until many years later that she told me that a man had exposed himself to her at some earlier stage in her life.

❖

My experience of growing up feels like growing into a kind of deformity, rather like one of those dry trees with withered branches that are bent by the strength of the prevailing wind and struggle to maintain a grip in the poor soil. They have never had the experience of growing gradually, tall and straight, in an enabling climate, pushing out leaves and becoming more and more themselves, feeling the juices flow.

There is a different image of myself that keeps recurring, of having a kind of wholeness like a poppy head, smooth, with a firm outer casing, seeming whole, but in a limited way and without connections with the wider wholeness that is there. This image feels very constrained, self-contained. It leads on to other associations: of suddenly breaking open and everything pouring out, of pregnant possibilities, of Pandora's box, of an empty husk being left behind.

Another image is of a small, pink, helpless, soft centre (a baby?) that has been enclosed by a shell or wall and is now, because the wall is coming down, becoming increasingly exposed and vulnerable and needs to be cared for.

❖

Dad and I kept our distance. I know he adored me and was proud of what I achieved in life. It was a simple love, that couldn't express itself fully and in the open, but I knew it was there, and it was a kind of bedrock. I loved him so much but I didn't say this, the cool wary person I became precluded it. And yet, I dare to hope that, just as I know he cared deeply for me, but in a significant way was not there for me, as a father, when I needed him as a child, so he, also, knew that behind the cool facade was a daughter who loved him and valued him.

❖

Chronologically, my spiritual life and my sexual life started at a rather similar time. I realized that an erection was attached to sexual thoughts and fantasies, and at the same time I started struggling with those thoughts and fantasies which I regarded as 'evil'.

I regarded them as evil because I knew that many of them were not normal. But I am not sure how I knew that. No one told me they were not normal, but I knew I could not talk about them. Perhaps it was because no one else talked about having those kinds of desire, even in jest, that I realised that I would be saying something simply irreversible if I did talk about them. Perhaps it was the book in the library, *Love without fear*, which told me such desires were bad (it certainly confirmed it); or perhaps it was just my own sense of what is right and what is wrong.

Whatever was the cause of my feeling about my own sexuality, it was reflected most strongly in my interests in poetry. The poet whom we were, coincidentally, studying in our literature classes was T. S. Eliot. I was particularly impressed by *The waste land*, in which there is a passage concerning the sexual relationship between a man and woman. Theirs is an 'arid' meeting, empty of love, but mechanically sexual. Eliot's alternative is faith; it became mine too.

The odd thing is that while this 'spirituality' certainly lacked depth and was never properly explored, being rather more literary and artificial than real, it was strong enough to affect my sexual development. So, though in one way there was no real conflict in me, as I went on thinking sexy thoughts anyway, in another way I still held back sexually. I still felt deeply, from somewhere, that sex was not straightforward in some way, not simply to be enjoyed.

This was why I did not masturbate until I was over twenty. In reality the first urges to masturbate had come on me unawares when I was in my early teens – a strange pleasant sensation when moving in my bed while waiting to go to sleep. The next day I felt a little sore, and so I did not do it again, and the moment passed. So, by the time I knew what masturbation was, it had become my own spiritual *cause célèbre.*

❖

Nudity was a highly charged subject to me throughout childhood and adolescence. I never dared to have a communal bath or shower after gym or games at school; it was just too scary. I was frightened of having an erection in public. Yet it was very attractive at the same time. One of the other boys at school showed me a nudist magazine, and that became a regular source of erotic interest for me during my teens. Most of the pictures were carefully airbrushed, so they were rather misleading. I found the pictures of men more interesting but I had no idea why. My sexual feelings remained very private and compulsively autoerotic. Masturbation was irresistibly pleasurable. My feelings of guilt were almost omnipresent, but they were never strong enough to stop me for more than a few days, however much I tried. Masturbation was not something talked about in my school, at least not among those that I mixed with. I couldn't conceive that any or all of the other boys were having similar experiences.

❖

I was aware of my sexuality but it seemed to have no place in the world I inhabited. As the epistles of Paul, so often declaimed from the pulpit, reminded me, the body was unclean, the route to sin. I was not at ease with my body, so seldom encountered in the unheated houses of my childhood, but it felt good and fascinated me. In the bath and in bed I masturbated but the pleasure was mixed with fear and guilt. This seemed only proper. 'Never again!' I wrote firmly in my Letts diary, in a futile attempt to convince myself that it was possible to reform.

Girls were a complete mystery. Good to be with, desirable certainly, but inscrutable. It was up to me to do something, but what? It was impossible to know what they would welcome. Some would let me hold their hand but refused a proffered kiss, others would kiss with great enthusiasm but refused to walk hand in hand. And the terrible shame and confusion of getting it all wrong! In my imagination, girls were welcoming and attracted to me. In reality, I was unsuccessful and my affection was shown up for what it really was – unbridled lust.

My confusion was complete. It never occurred to me that the girls were as confused as I was, that they didn't know what to do either. It was impossible to talk about the problem with them and with my parents unthinkable. They just wouldn't understand. They couldn't have experienced anything like this. They were good. The problem was mine alone and I had to deal with it.

❖

For me, my parents lie outside the sexual arena.

❖

My first experience of loving – if that was what it was – was when I was 14, and was with a girl (I shall call her Julie) who was in my class. I was never aware of any real response from her. I used endlessly to inspect what was happening, interpreting every look, every choice of where to sit in lessons, in the light of my overwhelming wish that she would respond.

On one occasion, a group of us went to a party, and she and I were, temporarily, separated from the others, who had got ahead of us. I suppose I walked alongside her, trying to think of some way of making her say something, or of saying something to the purpose myself (without being too much to the purpose). I can imagine that I held my hand at my side, hoping for a touch of her hand. I think I remember her saying something like 'We'd better join the others' and me saying 'Do we have to? – yes of course...'

I started telling myself stories of how it would all be. One went like this: I would see her after school, perhaps late in the library. And we would walk out of school together, and we would walk along the road toward the stop where she caught her bus. And always, through some simple chemistry, we would be holding hands by the time we got to such and such a place, and we would kiss...

At this time, I must have been experiencing my first really strong sexual feelings, which were far from 'romantic'. I could hardly have put the two together in any way, because my feelings about Julie were so innocent. Kissing, even, was an unknown quantity, though I felt it must be absolutely the height of love to kiss. But, in a sense, kissing (in my imagination) was not a physical event, or, at least, not a sexual physical event, but an aesthetic event – the last frame of the film, or chapter of the novel.

❖

During my adolescence in the early 1950s I remember thinking to myself that marriage was something you were not allowed a second try at. You had to get it right first time, and if you didn't you simply had to make the best of it. You were supposed to be sexually chaste until the marriage ceremony was behind you. Somehow you were supposed to make a transition from being a self-controlled teenager who never overstepped the mark, to participating in the joys and duties of life-long Christian marriage, and you were supposed to do this with virtually no practical training.

Two of my classmates, neither of them considered 'loose' or 'wild' or 'daring', and both likeable, had to get married when they were about 16 or 17 because the girl was pregnant. As far as I can remember, I think the rest of the class was surprised, perhaps a bit shocked, but not condemnatory. The two had overstepped the mark set by society, and they had to pay the price of marriage for it. Christianity appeared to have little to say to teenagers about sexuality apart from 'no'.

❖

I am sixteen. I dream I am married. I am a bird flapping my wings against the bars of a cage. Waking from this dream is like walking away from prison.

I am thirty-six. Yesterday a friend asked me how I had escaped. She was referring to marriage. By my dreams, I said.

❖

I had very little incentive to play The Game. The rewards didn't interest me, I didn't need them enough.

Playing The Game and being successful meant going out with boys and getting accepted by the group of girls who went out (and slept) with boys. The boys scared me, the girls bored me, the rules seemed complicated and the competition tough. I could either play and risk failing (or scraping by), or I could choose to be absent, simply not turn up. I chose to be absent.

So, I was absent, not only from The Game, but from myself. My game was invisible. I had no language by which to explain to myself the passion I felt for another woman. I could not interpret my own desires. All I knew was that my desires were not reflected in any part of The Game the other girls were playing.

Being absent from The Game, I have had no way of telling where I've been or where I've arrived – no rites of passage. Sometimes I turn round quickly, hoping to glimpse something like the wake left by a boat so that I can watch the shape my life has been making as I've grown up. But there are few signs to mark the transition points from one phase of my life to another. There are no equivalents to Engagement, Marriage or Childbirth; few opportunities for public celebration.

Being absent was a lonely experience. I have an image of myself trying to find my way through the maze of those years. It is a maze of gauze curtains, nothing is distinct or clearly formulated, just vague shapes, dim outlines which I followed as instinctively and sometimes as desperately as an animal searches for food. Relationships with men began happening to me in spite of myself: I never felt I had chosen them. I simply reacted to the effects of them and longed for something else. By the time I woke up to the pain of isolation, more than 10 years had passed.

❖

Between the ages of 14 and 19 I fell in love passionately three times, and always with women. Since then my sexual relationships have all been with men, but I still have deep and intense feelings for women friends. Looking back, what strikes me most forcibly is that the quality and intensity of my feelings for my women loves was the same as it has been for the men in my life. I suppose this is why I have never been able to understand why people get so worked up about homo-, hetero- or bi-sexuality. With my heart and my guts I know that love is one, that sexual passion is the same whether the beloved object is of the same sex or a different one.

Because I had so little to identify with in terms of my own feelings, I had been in love with three male friends before I realised that I was homosexual. It only gradually dawned on me that the passionate attachment I felt to these three friends was what heterosexuals called love. All three men were heterosexual. In any case, I was too inhibited to make any sexual moves and didn't have my first physical relationship until I was twenty-five. This was not just a physical experience, but one of the most profound and passionate involvements of my life. Despite the law and the Judaeo-Christian tradition I could not believe that anything as beautiful as this could be wrong. We were not able to form a long-term sexual relationship for many reasons, and this caused me a lot of turmoil and grief for some years. However, we still keep in touch with one another despite the years, the distance, and my friend's marriage.

During the early 1960s this falling in love, combined with other problems, led me to go for psychotherapy with a Jungian-trained therapist. I can't remember now how long I went to her – I think it may have been a couple of months, or possibly less. In the course of this therapy I was given suggestions about how I might begin to change my patterns of life and orientation. At this point it became crystal-clear to me that I did not want to change my personality, and I accepted my sexual orientation for what it was.

I have never found it easy to make contact through pubs and clubs. I don't like the smoke, the noise and the drink and find it hard to chat up people I don't know. But my sexual needs didn't go away. I decided to try out the Turkish baths and found welcome physical relief, sometimes warmth, friendliness and mutual consideration. I know I'm not the only Quaker to have started a long-term sexual relationship in a sauna.

❖

For better or for worse, erotica has a significant part in my life. There are some fantasies and practices that do not turn me on, that I perhaps find repellent, but there are others that I find exciting and beautiful. I find sado-masochistic stories problematic because actual pain to myself would turn me off sexually, but the stories imply that both the slave and the master receive a deep satisfaction and achieve a kind of transcendent closeness. I can't quite project myself into the position of loss of self-control in a situation of mutual trust that the slave needs to gain sexual release. The inflicting of pain is something I have no interest in. But part of the aim of erotica is to sexualize the nooks and crannies of life rather than restricting sex to the bedroom and the night. Eric Gill wrote somewhere that he thought men (at least) thought about sex a lot of the time in the interstices of work and other activities, and I think that's true.

❖

There are many things I haven't written about: sexual fantasies (mine tending to be masochistic and with incestuous overtones). As for masturbation, my confession is that I'd probably rather read a good book. There's a whole lot of stuff about not being in touch (!) with my body, and even more about not liking it.

I have a very clear remembrance of an occasion in Meeting when an elderly man, visiting the meeting, got up and sang:

> Spirit of the living God, fall afresh on me,
> Spirit of the living God, fall afresh on me,
> Break me, melt me, mould me, fill me,
> Spirit of the living God, fall afresh on me,

As I sat in meeting I found myself feeling very angry. The imagery in what had been sung I found very unacceptable, i.e. a dominant person doing what he liked with the other. When I had heard those words as a young person I had always had the image of a potter moulding a pot out of pliant clay. Hearing them again, when my mental/spiritual set was so different, I found myself relating to the words in terms of relationships, including that with God. My experience, by then, was of relationships being much more to do with something reciprocal and involving equality and mutual respect.

But I do have another more sexual image which contradicts what I have just written. It is the image of Torvill and Dean as they danced their set piece at the 1984 Olympics. The dance was to do with the man as the toreador with the woman as the cape. The man was very dominant, masterful, eventually throwing the cape down in a final climactic finish. I found the imagery very attractive. Oh to have a masterful man! The music was pretty good too. This does leave me pretty confused. Do I want to be part of a relationship where I am done to or do I want to be part of a relationship where I can initiate, reciprocate and respond? Perhaps the answer is both.

She was saying that all pornography should be banned, because it causes men to abuse women. Particularly she said that pornography that shows the humiliation of women by men should be banned.

And I found myself saying to myself that she needed to be humiliated.

I caught myself saying this, and clamped down upon my own thoughts immediately. Yet, I could not expunge the trace of that thought from my mind. Nor what it told me about myself.

Any kind of sexual practice which means the forcible involvement of one party is anathema to me for myself and certainly for anyone I love, but it is quite clear that many, many people by their own choice take part in practices which I wouldn't want for myself. In my twenties I found the thought of sado-masochistic sex (between consenting adults) mildly exciting. Now I don't. I don't know whether it is because of advancing years, the cooling of the blood or too much knowledge via the media of real torture in the world but I find it hard to remember that I once thought it exciting, though I know I did.

❖

I'm beginning to be cautious with my own disgust because I wonder what it hides or suppresses in me. I know a lot (if not all) we find annoying about others is reflected somewhere in ourselves, our shadow that we fail or refuse to own. Perhaps it's the same with 'disgust', although the reflection of it may be more insidious and hidden.

❖

I can best describe the experience of my relationship with this woman as being like being hungry and unable to feed satisfactorily. While I was telling my friends that she could take my breath away, sometimes, with the way she looked, and even trying to say to them that I was waiting to see whether my feelings would develop into 'love' or not, there was a dislocation between what I was talking about and the reality. I knew it, and yet I did not know it.

I have never been able simply to look into myself and ask: Do I feel any response to this expression of affection which this person is directing at me? Instead, I start off by accepting that person's love, and reciprocating it, at least in a superficial way, taking what is 'on offer'. And then later I find that I do not actually reciprocate it at all. I find that there is absolutely nothing there.

Because we are not trained to express our sexual desires verbally – and there is some risk in so doing – we tend to expect the other person to sense what we want without our actually having to say it. Probably many people have too restricted a repertoire of giving and taking sexual pleasure with their partners, but often it may be damaging to the other person to express our aversions or reluctances. Or rather we may feel it to be damaging.

I had developed as a public communicator in both the written and spoken word. But I was not as proficient in communicating my feelings, my inner life, my intimate emotions to my wife and others. I was/am sensitive and felt/feel emotions keenly, but I had been given few skills to be able to make sense of them and to communicate them so as to receive feedback and help. In some aspects of development and growth I was isolated, separated, battling away on my own. It is only relatively recently that I have been able to get more in touch with my emotions and feel able to expose them to others and be strong enough to make myself vulnerable. I think that this is part of my conditioning as a male – particularly from my background where the macho thing is to be tough-minded, independent and self-reliant. I wonder how many other men relate to this aspect of male conditioning that needs to be (and is being) broken down to allow more authentic and close relationships to develop.

I feel I grew up with a lot of emotional reference points missing. Since many emotions were hidden from me (by my parents) I couldn't make the connections, via language, to my own experience: I couldn't express much of my own emotional experience directly with confidence or congruence.

I have discovered that there is a strange circularity and interdependence between language, feeling and behaviour. Becoming able to express, to speak my love in turn increased my capacity to believe in it and feel it. Equally, the clearer the feeling became, the more open and confident was my expression of it. If I don't use my joy, my love, my grief, I lose the use of my passion, like a muscle which is not exercised, my capacity for passion is diminished.

The Hebrew prophets knew that the gift of passion was to be used. Moreover, they knew that the effects (both personal and political) would be far-reaching if it wasn't. The prophets knew that if the people lost their capacity to express their passion for their God and for their Promised Land they would lose everything. The people would then cease to be the children of God, the Chosen Ones, and through sheer indifference they would become victims of the forces of greed and lust for power, which raged all around their little country, and which still rage around us today.

❖

People like me whose experience of mothering was not 'good enough' struggle always, and I feel sure that the relationship that I have had in my marriage redeemed me. When I got married I didn't believe it could last but it has, and it has got better. It was a bit – looking back – like moving from some bleak, rocky, northern territory to a country where the sun shone. I have been incredibly affirmed in this relationship and with my children, and have come to acknowledge some things of worth in myself. I do not know where I would have been without this partnership.

But the framework of strength and certainty, which has been so important, is something which I am now experiencing as restrictive. After many years of 'fitting in' to a safe haven, I have become a more challenging and less comfortable person to live with. I have changed and I am committed to more change. My emotional self-sufficiency is being dented and I am finding a stronger sense of self. I feel that I am expanding, breaking out of a carapace, becoming aware of hidden, neglected shadow parts of myself.

❖

I have to learn to face the hard truth that no relationship, no person, can be 'owned' or kept forever, that loss is a part of life and something to be reckoned with. At the same time I am trying to learn to believe that loss is not necessarily the substance of life, neither is it the sole outcome or fruit of my attempts to love. This takes immense courage.

❖

Confronting our uncertainties

The image of respectability that Quakers enjoy in society at large is not always a comfortable thing to live with. How often we hear the comment 'I'm not good enough to be a Quaker' said by someone who is neither better nor worse than we are! In talking to each other in the group about our uncertainties with regard to sex, we've tried to let go our fears about feelings and experiences that run the whole gamut between respectability and its opposite, believing that we needed to know each other and be known in as much honesty as we could summon. This has taken time and courage.

While we have listened to each other non-judgementally, the process has at times resembled the catharsis of confession. Each of us has been aware how much we need forgiveness from God, each other and not least ourselves. Encountering each other in our vulnerability has taught us that, paradoxically, mutual respect flows from honesty and risk-taking and not from the conventionally respectable. On numberless occasions we have experienced how this sharing in an atmosphere of trust has a deep healing quality.

I expect that intimate relationships (especially exclusive, sexual relationships) will always be fearful as well as joyful experiences for me. I can't wipe out the effects of my past. I think I shall always fear loss: I will instinctively look for guarantees of safety, or withdraw into my shell when I feel I have invested too much of myself emotionally in someone who may leave me.

It is one of the problems of my life that I am scared of upsetting people, and my mother's capacity for being upset meant that I stopped telling her things I thought might upset her. Of course there are two sides to this – her being upset and my inability to cope with that. I felt that my mother was setting me standards of behaviour or expectation that were difficult for me to achieve. I knew without her having to say very much that there were things in which I was deficient. Shall I ever forget the occasion on which I swore (rather mildly) at being asked to go to see my aunt down the road? Yet my mother was not an authoritarian or demanding person. Nonetheless I can see in retrospect that

I sought out and valued a variety of substitute mother-figures in the two or three decades after my adolescence, women with whom I felt emotionally more comfortable than with my mother.

❖

Respectability is not a personal burden if one is living in a way which is acceptable to others and to oneself. I am in that position now, and it certainly makes life easy, and gives greater emotional space to devote to concerns other than purely personal ones. But of course, like everyone else, there have been times when I have felt that I have behaved in a far from 'respectable' manner, in the way in which this is generally understood. The main burdens I felt then were connected with the need for secrecy, since otherwise I would have had to admit publicly that I was not living up to my own self-imposed standards of not harming (or potentially harming) others.

❖

I suffer from being the classic middle-class professional woman who has a home, children, husband, etc. and who also wishes to give time to things that interest her. In the process of trying to do well all the things with which I am involved I get very tired, particularly at certain points in the year. Advice usually comes in the form of suggesting that I give up the things that interest me rather than work or domestic chores. I choose to continue but the cost is there.

There is also the personal cost of examining myself in a way that I perhaps have not before and of sharing things that I had assumed were safe in their secrecy. As I think about my secrets which destroy the conventional societal image that I assume most people have of me, not least my husband and children, I am afraid. The fear is to do with the possible loss/cost in my personal relationships. When I fell passionately in love with another man in my early thirties it almost destroyed my husband and my marriage because I did not keep it secret. Is there really safety in secrecy? Might the risk of openness be too great?

We began attending Quakers shortly after, joining about a year later. Now, thirteen years later, the cement of Quakerism which undoubtedly held our marriage together is cracking. Whether this is in the foundations or just a settlement crack remains to be discovered. I find it interesting that I am using a house as a metaphor for my marriage. Houses have so often featured in my dreams and they have certainly been a major part of my personal security.

❖

As a parent it was a privilege to be for a time a 'keeper of my children's temporary helplessness'. I found it necessary, though, continually to let go so that gradually my influence changed and in many respects became increasingly redundant. It is a difficult and risky balance to try and give appropriate support on the one hand, and on the other genuinely to accept their growing independence, especially in the sexual field – although looking back I very rarely found trust betrayed.

I don't like sex that is done in order to degrade or humiliate someone else or to use them or their presence against their will. But as a man, I haven't come across much of that. I understand that most women have had the experience of men exposing themselves in frightening or embarrassing circumstances. In reading about sado-masochistic experiences or fantasies those that upset me are the ones where the fantasy is about permanent or long-term enslavement, of one person being totally at the will of another. In real life I personally would become frightened by pain.

I have occasionally been involved in sex without fully wanting it. I mean, I've got into a situation without really being clear about it and just let it happen, because it would have been too awkward or embarrassing to stop it. That sort of thing leaves me feeling unhappy with myself. It's a kind of self-disgust at being lukewarm and uncommitted.

Very many people with illnesses such as HIV or AIDS feel alienated, outcasts cut off from normal human society. In the face of the losses, actual or potential, which pile up in the course of illness – loss of health, of strength, of work, of sex, of income, of friends, of home, of independence, of choice, of life itself – one can quickly feel stripped of everything that gives one any sense of self-worth.

One's sexuality is a very fundamental part of one's being, and of one's self-image. Unlike those who have most other illnesses, many people with AIDS have the further burden of traditional Christian teaching that homosexual acts are intrinsically sinful. Being taught that one's innate bodily responses and sexuality are sinful does not give one a good basis for building loving, creative, intimate relationships. This is a problem for some heterosexuals too. It is but a short step from this to the feeling that AIDS is God's punishment. The popular press does not often print the gospel (good news) that enlightened Christian teaching is about a God who suffers alongside us, and helps us transcend loss and suffering.

My daughter is bisexual. She has loved both a man and a woman. She is a super young woman whom I love dearly and admire enormously for her honesty and integrity. She is not promiscuous, in fact she is the very opposite. When she told me about her bisexuality I felt both affirmed and sad. Although what she told me was news it was as if I had known it for a long time. I think we are closer for the recognition I have of her sexuality. The sadness is tied in with anger because I know that life will be harder for her as she seeks to be true to her sexual self. She will be on the receiving end of prejudice, ignorance and bigotry, not least among some Quakers and her own family. I would not wish anyone to be on the receiving end of discriminatory and oppressive attitudes and certainly not my lovely daughter.

I am visiting Anna. We are sitting close and talking calmly. I am just about to massage her feet when the phone rings. It is her lover. I know she has a lover. She is talking to him quietly. My stomach churns. I am resentful that our time together has been invaded. Perhaps I should be angry, but I feel I have no right to be angry just because someone has telephoned. Anna loves him I suppose. I believe she loves me too. But he is a man, I am a woman. Do I have the same rights to her love? Can I believe that I do? It takes enormous courage. Most of the time I enjoy loving her so much that I just want to forget about him, but I carry the subconscious awareness of him around with me, knowing he can pop up like this at any moment to haunt me just when I'm beginning to think it's safe to relax. Suddenly I am cold and shaking and throwing up in the loo because I'm afraid. I tell myself I shouldn't have risked this love, that it's too uncertain. I suddenly want to pull back all the bright strands of love I have thrown out to Anna. But I know it's too late. I have trusted her with my heart and I must trust what my heart tells me, because I know my life's not worth living if I can't.

Anna returns from the phone. I return from the loo. She apologises for the interruption. I could let it go at that, as if it was just an interruption, and pick up where we left off. But I can't. I'm going to tell her I'm scared, because I am. So, I do. And we stumble along for a while, vulnerable and awkward. Suddenly I'm not enjoying sitting here any more, having to reveal how her lover affects me. Suddenly I am wandering in a cold landscape alone, trying to find my way through a maze of disconnected words, blank, silent spaces and patches of dark, speechless fear. But, painful as it is, I am also relieved to be speaking these feelings because I hear myself come out with them: as they emerge I see more clearly who I am.

As we grope our way along, some semblance of order returns to my life. Panic subsides. She reassures me that she loves me, but this doesn't seem to be the point. I believe that she does love me. I'm just trying to find ways of making it safe for me to love her. Perhaps there is no safe way to love, only ways of listening to what I need as I love. So, I listen to what I need.

I tell her I need some time now to centre myself again. We sit opposite one another, turn off the lights and let ourselves sink into the candle-lit silence. Anna speaks of the vision she had a few days ago. It is a vision of light. I see the light burning inside my forehead as she speaks. I'm scared by the brightness of it. We are seeing the light reflected in each other. This is what our love is. We are incarnating it, re-membering it. We are both scared by it sometimes. I pray, thanking God for the light and the darkness, finally just letting everything be in the silence.

After this we lie down on the sofas opposite each other and talk, looking at each other across the glow of candle flame.

It's getting late. She offers me a taxi home. I say I'd be happy to sleep on the sofa. I've brought my toothbrush, just in case. She laughs. She is pleased I want to stay with her, she comes to embrace me and our bodies find their familiar warmth and comfort together.

In her dreams, I am putting oil on my hands, ready to give her a massage. In my dreams she is giving me a cake with fireworks on it.

❖

In the end, I began to look for women who appeared to know what they wanted – I thought of them as sexually experienced. If they were prepared to risk themselves, then I was prepared to risk myself too. Both my sexual relationships have started in this way. It was an undeserved gift that Pat, with whom I have shared my life ever since, although she seemed to be such a woman, underneath turned out to be as uncertain and vulnerable as I was. A much fuller and more rewarding relationship ensued. My hidden spirituality was eventually released.

I spent much of my life feeling inadequate because, according to the books, I didn't 'do it' properly. Perhaps here is the place to admit something I have never dared admit in the five years we have been together because I have felt so ashamed about it. I still fear that you will all despise me and think me odd. I have never masturbated. That took a great deal of courage to type.

I am at a party, standing on the edge of the dance floor. I am trying to decide whether to ask someone for a dance. But I do not want just to dance. I imagine the dancing leading to embraces, the embraces to sex. Part of me knows this to be a fantasy, that other scenarios – indifference or rejection – are more likely. Finally I do not ask her to dance. But the first fantasy remains an alluring possibility.

❖

I see her coming toward me, and see the curve of her thighs and hips (indeed, I don't see anything else of her, except, perhaps, a glimpse of her face) and I see the way she fills her clothes, and I know I want to turn round and look at her from behind as she passes me and goes on down the street between the other people, and I play with the idea of changing course and following her, and in the end I don't even turn round to look in case someone sees me doing it and jumps to the right conclusion...

I feel fantasy as something very powerful in my life and over which I have to keep tight rein. I am aware that on those occasions when I have 'fallen in love' it has always been when I have in some way consented to the experience, even when I most felt it to be an alien invading force sweeping me off my feet and leaving me no choice. I have in fact said 'yes' to this alien, however much I may have pretended to myself at the time that I had no control over it.

My being a Quaker very much affects my erotic life. I am conscious that much of the time I am censoring the erotic in my everyday life, because I am trying to be 'virtuous', by which I mean faithful to my partner in thought and fantasy as well as in deed. I have experienced the overwhelming power of the erotic and its capacity to blast apart all my hard-won tranquillity and I fear to be possessed by it. At the same time I know that when I am in the grip of sexual passion I feel alive as at no other time, so that part of me longs for the experience.

So there is a continual struggle in my inner self between the me who yearns for the excitement of learning about a new love in depth, and the awakened spiritual awareness that for me always accompanies that experience, and the me who longs for peace and tranquillity and to 'be good'. It is a true dichotomy because in the turbulent throes of sexual passion I am most open to spiritual insights, I work at my spiritual life in a way that I never do at any other time. Yet I am aware that what I am feeling would be rejected by most Quakers (and by my own personal censor too!) so that I feel guilty and troubled.

This leads me to censor my fantasy life, mainly I suppose for fear that thinking erotically about someone other than my partner will lead me to 'fall in love' with all the consequent potential for destructiveness of thought and behaviour.

There are very few people with whom I have ever been able to talk about fantasy or the erotic life that goes on in my head. I think I have never done so with lovers because I have felt that it would be too threatening to them. It is the one truly private area of my life, inaccessible even to myself much of the time, like a film that I catch a glimpse of out of the corner of my eye, occasionally sabotaged by my dreams which show me where my erotic fantasies are looking and I wake feeling guilty as if the desire and the action were one and the same.

Speaking rationally, for me as a Quaker, it would be permissible to have erotic fantasies about my partner, but not about anyone else. The sad corollary is that in a long-term settled relationship erotic fantasies are rare because they are of discovery, of penetrating (the sexual imagery is intentional) the veil surrounding the mystery of another human being.

❖

My overriding feeling was of tight, fearful, sexual excitement. I was in this state of excitement from the moment I woke. I was going to the sex shop: I was going to buy pornography with those pictures in it, ones I had often imagined for myself, and I was now going to buy them ready made.

To my surprise, when I arrived, in the middle of the day, the sex shop was closed for lunch. I suppose I could have gone home at that moment (was it a sign that I should?); but I did not. I think although my fear and excitement were mixed together, the excitement, and the challenge, had the greater weight.

But I was afraid of someone seeing and recognising me; I was also afraid of God. I was actualising, turning into reality, a sinful desire for an image, the resistance of which had functioned as a test for my spirituality. The desire for these images had been a test because they came from my 'dark' side against which my 'light' side was supposed to be struggling. And they came from my dark side because they turned me on. I might even have had an erection since I set out for the sex shop;

certainly I was aware of a compulsive power, stronger than any fear, of physical desire.

When a man came back from lunch to open the shop, I was first in. I was so nervous that I did not really take in what I could see; but I have the memory of an impression of smallness, and of there being walls with racks of magazines on them, and on these racks, large numbers of back issues stacked one behind the other. The prices seemed to me outrageously high. Two other men came in. This increased my nervousness – I felt they were looking at me.

There was quite a selection of the kind of magazine I was looking for; and I was not clear whether it was OK to look through them or not. And always I sensed how awful it was that I was admitting that I was interested in these images, that I 'needed' them. (Perhaps, in other circumstances, admitting as much would be regarded as enlightened.)

I glanced at a few magazines, and chose two; but I was shaking so much that I could hardly get the money out to pay for them. Nor did I feel I could question the fact that I was charged a higher price even than what was indicated on the covers. I seem to remember saying 'Thanks, mate' as the proprietor gave me the change. What was that false confederacy there for? I felt it was false. Perhaps it was not.

When I got back to my room, I got the magazines out and masturbated whilst looking at their pictures; I can still recall the images, and would recognise them immediately if ever I saw them again.

It was only after I had masturbated that a wave of self-revulsion overwhelmed me. Even then, I don't think it hit me immediately, but came up, and grew slowly. It was as powerful in its way as the drive to buy the magazines had been beforehand. I felt I could not keep the things, that I must get rid of them. At this moment of self-disgust, fear of discovery, and guilt, I remember an image in my mind of a long black cloud passing over me, with clear weather on either side, but somewhere else, not where I was. In the end, I acted in a most irrational and absurd way. I took the magazines outside, and walked up the road, and into an area of the town where there were fewer houses. Then I put the magazines down an open drain.

❖

Masturbation too fulfils the need at least. But for me, this feels prick-led, meaning that aspect of being a man which insists on seeing women as things not fellow creatures. I'm not proud of reading and enjoying pornography nor of the fantasies that assail me when meeting, or even simply passing on the street, an attractive woman. But this is a part of me, an occasion for sin, perhaps, but nonetheless an aspect I have to try to integrate and live with, as best I can.

❖

The woman and I were sexually attracted to one another, though my emotional involvement was probably less than hers. She was very experienced sexually, but only after a considerable period did we begin, occasionally, to have sex. It was possible to talk to her, however, about my sexuality without fear of her judgement or disapprobation. Instinctively, I felt it would be no problem to speak to her about my sexual desire to play sado-masochistic games, for her understanding of the way role-play could be a part of love-making suggested to me that she would not regard my desire as disgusting, and would not reject me as a result of knowing of it. When I told her about my desire, I did not do so as a confession; and so it was that she began to fulfil the desires my sexuality thrust upon me.

Although having sex has frequently made me feel guilty, I never felt guilty about playing with her the games which fulfilled these particular desires, she never made me feel guilty about it. Nor did she use the power my desires had over me – though she knew of that power I am sure. She seemed, herself, excited by my excitement. But, possibly, she might have felt that to refuse to 'play' would have been to risk the relationship. There was an agreement that we would refrain from these games if she so desired; but that was never put to the test.

One thing does seem clear to me, and that is that engaging in sexual intercourse with another person does change the nature of the relationship, sometimes in ways that you can't anticipate. Do I say this, though, because our culture has invested the couple relationship with such a powerful aura that it has made it, in most circumstances, impossible to regard sexual activity between two people as an amoral activity? Am I simply the kind of person that is so hung-up about sex that I can't regard sexual intercourse as on a level with, say, sharing a meal with someone, having a good conversation or playing a game of tennis? What makes sex different?

❖

There can be difficulties when personal and professional boundaries and public and the private boundaries get muddled. When a student fell in love with me I tried to turn what was personal and private into something professional and private, in order to help. At the same time I maintained the public and professional role as a lecturer. It would have been easier and far less frightening just to have ignored and rejected the personal approach and advised the seeking of help elsewhere. I must say I was enormously relieved when the course was over. We are now very good friends although not in quite the same way that I am friends with other people. I cannot say what the difference is exactly except that it had to do with the possibility of sexual intimacy and the depth of sharing.

❖

The exceeding sinfulness of sin (Romans 7:13) is unfashionable in Quaker ministry nowadays. Until recently the concept was tied up in my mind with a lot of things like lust and gluttony, avarice and sloth; and it was especially connected with sex. These I knew to be the bad side of things which are valuable, like sexual love and good food, thrift and leisure. 'Sin' brought to my mind pompous and narrow-minded people telling me (through pursed lips) how bad I was. It is easy to reject the notion of sin; but something central to centuries of traditional Christian wisdom must be talking about a real state of human consciousness. However, as John Wilhelm Rowntree points out (*Christian faith and practice*, ¶94), the Christian religion does not consist in refraining from things which are done by other people.

I have begun to realise that sin is a sense of inner emptiness, of worthlessness, of separation from God and from one's community. It is a common experience in the journals of early Friends: the inward light is said first to act like a searching light, showing up sin before leading out of it. Jungians might call it the encounter with the shadow. Perhaps it is an early stage on any real inward or spiritual journey.

What then of those things that are popularly understood as sin? Avarice, gluttony, lust, pride, envy, anger, sloth are the usual list, the seven deadly sins. These are human attempts to assuage the different forms that the torment of feeling empty and worthless takes. They all have in common that they numb the pain of isolation temporarily, but then the relief wears off. They can all become habits which are difficult to break. What one of us does not feel such compulsions in response to neediness in some aspect of life? If you don't recognise this experience in yourself, I wonder if you need to look closer at pride. They seem to me secondary – attempts to fill a void which can only be fulfilled by the love of God – usually incarnated in, and mediated by, one's fellow human beings.

Do we start from the position that some behaviour must be unacceptable? I would like to question this assumption. Should we apply moral rules to other people's behaviour? We know our own limits, certainly, but can we apply them safely to others? There are two things dangerous in this procedure. The first is that we cannot know the circumstances which apply to others (we are not always very sure of those that apply to ourselves!). If X leaves his wife or Y is found to be having a sexual relationship with a pupil, it may seem obvious that harm is being done or there is exploitation in a relationship. But it is possible that the wife has been belittling X sexually for a number of years or even that Y's pupil actively sought the relationship.

The second danger is that problems in relationships are seldom as simple as they seem. It may be convenient to assume that there are only two parties involved but there are always others, parents, children, friends. To ask, for instance, that no action be taken that involves hurt to another is often impossible. And once we say that a little hurt is inevitable but that intention to hurt is the important thing, then we are off down the slippery slope of quantifying the unquantifiable and judging the unjudgeable.

A lot of what we have been doing is very meaningful in Quaker terms but there is much that challenges the rather neat healthy-mindedness of Friends, an orthodoxy that reveals itself in an unwillingness to confront the dark in ourselves and others. We are coming from deep places where many Friends do not like to go, and offering to Friends what Jung called, 'the precious gift of doubt', a gift which they may be reluctant to receive.

Celebrating our sexuality

Sexuality is embedded in the totality of who we are. It is inextricably mixed with our sense of self, with self-acceptance and self-worth. It forms a strand in all our relationships. In celebrating our sexuality, we are both giving thanks for one of God's greatest gifts and rejoicing in the ability to make contact with others at the deepest level, to know them in things eternal as well as temporal. It is no accident that in the writings of the mystics, as in the Song of Songs, *the soul's union with God is expressed in sexual terms.*

The way I met him is a most unexpected and wonderful example of God's loving care in my life. We fell in love and discovered Quakers at about the same time. Shortly afterwards, there was a wedding in our Meeting House. We did not know the couple, but we were welcomed to attend by a wise elder and by the groom. We sat and gave thanks for the gift of each other, cried a few tears and wondered at the beauty of a Quaker wedding. We held hands at the back of someone else's wedding, and there to our surprise we too 'very sensibly felt the Lord with us and joining us'. The 'sense of it has remained with us' to this day.

I'm not sure whether or not we want a wedding at this stage in our life together. The inward spiritual reality of marriage we have already. I do not know what an outward and visible sign would add; but many couples – including Quaker ones – have found that they are upheld by the overt recognition and support of their community which is shown in a Meeting for Worship or a civil or religious marriage ceremony. 'The simple Quaker wedding ... is the most natural expression of the way of life in which we believe.' I hope that some day those gay couples who might find it 'of good service' will be able to have a Quaker wedding of their own.

And so to marriage. I didn't want a child. (I guess I needed to look after my own inner child.) A scare, thinking I was pregnant, threw me into a panic.

Five years of marriage brought about a lot of healing and when I next thought I was pregnant I felt as if this was what I had been born for. We were in the States. It was 1962 and the doctor was dismissive, almost derisory, saying lots of women were missing periods because of anxiety over the Cuban missile crisis. Stupid, patronising man. I knew. My body knew. After an initial period of being queasy and falling asleep all over the place, I felt extraordinarily and intensely myself. A spotting of blood one day threw me into blind panic as I felt I might lose this child. The danger passed, though each of my pregnancies produced this phenomenon almost as if I were being tested and, each time, I had the same awful reaction. Being pregnant was wonderful. I recall that time with amazing vividness. I saw clearly as if for the first time. Everything was heightened. I can remember the clothes I bought, the walk each day to the university where I was working, the scents, the flowers. I could hardly stop from skipping up and down. It was Eros flowing everywhere. I was at home in my skin as never before.

And then the birth. I wake in the night aware that something is happening. The contractions are not regular, not tremendously strong, and I doze between them. I am in a kind of trance and, somewhere on the periphery, I am aware that I am being urged to go to the hospital. I feel very 'other', and quite detached, and don't see the need for this. I am where I am and this is all that matters. Eventually, as in a dream, we arrive at the impressive plate glass reception area at the hospital. I'm going at a snail's pace and watch with interest, and no embarrassment, as a pool of liquid gathers around my feet, spreads and snakes out in little tributaries. The baby is born an hour later.

Pregnant again in a few months. In contact with rubella. Abortion. Grief. Sick emptiness. I made the decision.

The other two pregnancies are wondrous times. I could go on having babies for ever. The births get quicker and easier. With the second, things happened so swiftly I couldn't get to the hospital and went down on all fours, panting like an animal ready to drop its young. With the third, the first twinge came at midnight. He was born an hour later.

Was there pain? Perhaps, but not as I've known it in other situations. It felt aweful, archetypal, with images of waterfalls and huge towering waves. I rode on the crest of the waves. I plunged, I flew, I was the world and the water. I was nothing. I was everything. I was a huge flower opening up, wider, wider, wider, until I must surely tear apart. I knew the meaning of everything.

And amidst the drudgery and mess of having a small child, there were other amazing moments. As I stand in the shower, the baby cries and milk flows from my breasts, faster and faster, forming little rivulets. I am completely taken over, embodying something far beyond me. I feel like a painting I have seen and the milk from my breasts goes out to make the Milky Way. Wet and slippery, I reach the crying child.

We connect.

What bliss.

❖

The bits of my story that I have not really told are to do with erotic and incestuous and lesbian and pornographic dreams. I am left with the thought that if I can dream of such things then they are part of me. Another area that I have not written about is masturbation from which I get a lot of satisfaction. It is part of the process of loving and accepting myself and that includes my body.

❖

Once, lying in bed in the dark, my hands roving, I suddenly produce the most amazing, wonderful, warm feeling of rapture, cleanness, liquefaction. I was so ignorant and so inhibited that I wasn't to evoke this sensation again for more than thirty years.

❖

I read recently that pre-pill women, of whom I am one, became very good at kissing because it was not safe to do much more. Certainly a lot of my early sexual experience involved prolonged intensive kissing, mostly with the lips at first and later with the tongue. I have always found kissing and the mouth to be intensely erotic both for me personally and watching others, particularly on film and television. I also find reading about kissing stimulating. I am sure a lot of this is related to early childhood experiences of sucking and feeding and finding out about the world with the mouth and hands. One of my most erotic experiences as an adult mirrored that experience of sucking and being fed and discovering the other person's lips and mouth with my fingers and later with my lips.

❖

It was, she said, as if a bolt of sexual electricity had passed between us – we both felt it, though we were not even holding hands at the time, and were just sitting there talking to some other people. It's because I know she is wearing the things I like and she knows I like and she likes me to like; and it is because she is going to be mine in just half an hour, or so. Nothing will be disallowed, and everything will be allowed; she knows what I like, and she plays with me. Who knows who has the power? I like her astride me, talking to me, telling me she will make me wait, moving her body as if it were a stroking hand. This is what will happen in half an hour or so; and this sudden bolt is the preshock which is palpable, though no one but we two can feel it.

When we are together, bodies engaged inextricably, so that I no longer know (nor care) whose is which, time stands still. And with our escape from that straitjacket, we seem to fill all the space there is and there is no room for separateness, for being alone, for worrying what comes next, or how, or any of the daily cares that so beset us.

There are bodies, of course, and feeling and yearning and even thinking but all entangled, reunited. Bodies are transformed; spirits, souls, no longer outlawed, return to find each other. And it is good, wonderful, bliss – not mine, though, or yours. Being is altogether richer. Light, perceived but dimly through the glass of faith at other times, is here. Walking in the garden in the cool of the day could have been like this.

This is making love. This is how it is after many false starts, blind alleys, roadblocks and even the odd diversion. This is the best of times, when fondness and need and generosity come together mysteriously and create a celebration, a sacrament for our relationship. Twenty-five years of growth together, of trying to understand, of getting closer, of failing again, hasn't guaranteed success. We know now when we have made love but still not how to do it. No matter how hard we try, however many sex manuals we devour, grace still manages to surprise us.

There's been a lot of fucking too. It's good. I can't deny that there's enjoyment and affirmation and being able to please each other. And of course the room to play and the time to act out our fantasies, to be the people that we can't bring ourselves to be outside the magic space of the bedroom. What starts as fucking can also suddenly, miraculously, fall into that state which I have described as making love.

Afterwards, when time returns and that question – was it all right for you? – suddenly makes sense again, then is a special close time. This is a time alike for whispered endearments, for silly jokes and raucous laughter, for lying huddled together, for talking over those difficult things that you have somehow never got round to, for simply giving thanks.

It is then that I know for certain that living with you, that staying with you is neither a trap nor a mistake but that I truly have found a fellow pilgrim.

❖

Celebrations were usually private affairs, shared by a few women, or with just one. They were often spontaneous celebrations with food and songs, flowers and incense. They were the celebrations of women working together, loving each other, sharing dreams and helping each other grow.

Fathomless, fallow times we shared, when communion sprang up all round us, fresh and surprising as the green of summer grass. And sometimes I had the strangest feeling that we were celebrating more than we knew ... something not to be kept with rings or promises, but to be savoured in the moment, like a kiss I hope to remember in my old age.

Relationships were not characterised by institutions, but as far as possible by free choice and free will. Each relationship is unique, full of paradox and contradiction, refusing to be contained within the limitations of time and space. I am loved in dreams. I am touched by one I thought dead, my blood still carries loves long past and my face falls in the fold of them.

The reality, as I have come to experience and celebrate it with my friends and lovers, is that we all move around like colours in a kaleidoscope, intense and fragile. We are trying to learn about love, trying to keep talking and listening even when we hurt each other, trying to celebrate our places of divergence as well as convergence.

We form a family, not of blood ties, not belonging to a physical home, but a family with a common story. In our attempt to live honestly and justly, in trying to search out new ways of relating, new patterns for living as women in the world, we are forming an ethical community with its own norms and values. Commitment is measured not in terms of quantity of time spent together, but rather in terms of the degree of honesty we can risk sharing with each other, the amount of space we can risk giving each other to grow.

The ethic evolves as we do. It's not very neat, not very orderly to live in this way, in fact it's rather messy. There are lots of goodbyes and few rules. There is an internal consistency and coherence, but to see the pattern emerging one must live it, from the inside, with courage.

We met for the first time when she and my friend and I went to see *One flew over the cuckoo's nest.* I remember she cried, when the rest of us were laughing, at the character of the big Indian. We walked home from the cinema to my friend's room and no doubt had some tea or coffee, and I think we stayed late in his room, the three of us, talking. And I was already infatuated with her; I could not stop looking at her, and it was a pleasure looking at her. I remember the deepness of the sensation which was greater than that of any other sensation I had ever felt. And I do remember that it was not attended by any frustration or sense of missing, but on the contrary seemed to be its own fulfilment.

A few days later I got a call from my friend, and he said that she wanted to see me. So I turned up after a day of revising (I was doing exams throughout this period) and went to her room. Her room inside was like any other room in the hall of residence where she lived, but was somewhat separated from them in a corner of the building. As it was summer, we could have her window open, and hear the night and early morning and the sound of railway shunting yards, which seemed to go on all night.

She and I sat together in her room and talked. I remember she said she was frightened of getting old, and of losing the suppleness of her joints; of death. The idea of ghosts seemed deeply to upset her. Slowly she and I moved closer to each other, until she was sitting at my feet, leaning back against my legs, and I was stroking her hair, which was short and brown, with my fingers. She did not want me to go, though the time was now into the deepest part of the night. She had a glass of water in her hand, and she threw it over me, so I had to take off my shirt, and stay while it dried.

We went to bed together. She lay on her back, and I lay beside her, with my head on the pillow, until I could bear the closeness and the tension of being close to her no longer. Moving until I was looking down into her face, with a sweet agonizing pleasure of slowness, hoping, and almost knowing in my heart she would respond, I kissed her.

There was never any time when I judged her as she really was: she always remained mysterious. She was always just beautiful, and I never saw her in any other way.

When the sun came up, I found I was in a place I had never been before: literally, as I had never woken up in bed with a woman, and metaphorically, as I had never been in love before. With her I had my first experience of touching a woman and giving her an orgasm, of seeing a woman in her underwear, of lying down with a woman. I remember how she played with me, pretending not to want to kiss me, keeping her lips closed and turning her head away from me.

My love for her was endless, but not violent.

I did not feel the miserable tension of wanting sex, though I must surely have wanted her in a general sexual sense: I wanted her pressed against me, or gently lying against me. Sexual climax was not something I wanted; to express my feeling for her I did not feel the need of it; she offered to touch me, and I avoided the issue.

I left her room before breakfast, and walked back to my halls of residence, on the other side of the campus. The morning was warm, and the clouds high, and as I climbed up the steep hill from where she lived, I looked back down on the valley in which her halls were situated, and felt I had everything.

❖

If I can love you
Sometimes so deeply
Sometimes so effortlessly
Sometimes so reluctantly
Sometimes so achingly
How you must bathe in the love
And light and power of angels and God;
How they must celebrate you
As a source and centre of light
On this still dim and dusky planet.

When I join in, through and with you
We can light up the world with our love.

With my body I worship you
With my mind I embrace you
With my emotions I sink deep inside you
With my spirit I gently brush against you.

To be together in our separateness
Is a gift
From the boundlessness
Of the Divine
– A reflection of her love.
And the light became flesh ...
... And we lived it.

Being a woman is changing my mind; is not feeling safe on the streets at night; is being at risk. Being a woman is being confused; is seeing myself distorted and disturbed; knowing all the definitions are up for grabs, so what the hell: anything's possible now. Is it? Being a woman means taking 40 years to believe in myself. Being a woman means not being a man; means being 'not a man' therefore invisible, seen through. Being a woman means being child-free, not comprehending women who want children, coming from a planet where that wasn't part of the plan. Being alien. Being a woman means loving women, mostly; means having a vagina, a cervix and a clitoris to be sucked and stroked – and here I come, caressed and spilling out of dreams, tasting of salt. Being a woman is searching beyond the boundaries of what is possible for women to know, stepping out beyond the definitions. Choosing choice. Being a woman means having breasts and soft cheeks and travelling light with my rucksack and my arms free; means running my pen across a blank page making it up as I go; means buying roses for myself and black underwear and high-heels and praying to an erotic God who wants to bless me. Being a woman means stretching myself to meet the future while my feet are stuck in the past. Being a woman means being stretched; means conceiving the impossible; means sitting on the loo, whistling, deciding to take my life into my own hands. Being a woman, running to the edge, the ledge, preparing to fly; being on the brink, each one of us a first. Go for it!

JUMP!

Being a woman is changing the world.

❖

I have found that sex can just be comfortable togetherness. There have also been wonderful times when orgasm felt like a profound sharing of my essence and receiving of another's; when love literally and symbolically flowed within and between us.

There have been times when, unbidden and unexpected, there has entered in the ecstacy of the climax a fleeting, yet tangible taste of a higher consciousness. As if, paradoxically, the eternal is touched in time.

For me, sex at its most profound is one way in which I can experience the energy which is creativity, healing, love, the living force, God.

❖

I wake slowly and wriggle in the comfort of the large bed. It is early and the person next to me still sleeps. I turn and examine the dear face on the pillow. I have known it so long and yet it can still surprise and delight me. The familiar contours with the lovely lips. We have shared a lot together: children growing up, family occasions, moving house too often, my parents dying, loving each other and hurting each other. I lean over and gently kiss the soft, tender skin at the temple. As he wakes I say, 'Hello my love, I'll get the coffee.'

❖

I didn't have high expectations of marriage, feeling that living so close to another person year in year out would be sure to bring sameness and disillusionment. But I was wrong, resoundingly and totally wrong. For my marriage has been an amazing gift.

Even in the dark, trying times – and there are those and they will continue – I know that this is where I want to be, and that any alternative existence, simpler though it might be, is just not on. We have made this commitment which remains: we love, we laugh, we fight and we know each other deeply.

There is sex at the heart of this. Sometimes its just a matter of a good fuck – basic, uncomplicated, cleansing (why is it that sex is so often thought of as dirty?). At other times it is a dance, a poem, a sacrament. In the morning, at night (and oh the luxury of love in the afternoon!). And the special joy of not having sex, of cuddling up together in bed, familiar bodies intertwined, close and comfortable. And the gentle affectionate touch in passing, the look across a crowded room, the shared silent laughter, clearing up together after dinner guests have gone and talking over the evening.

And after a quarrel, when harsh words have been hurled across the room like missiles, and frightening, 'unforgivable' things said; and after the cold, heavy, total silence that follows and feels even worse, then, magically, miraculously, comes reconciliation, and the amazing recognition that we have not 'blown it', that what we have forged together remains (is strengthened?), and love and delight spring again.

As I write this, I look forward, warm with anticipation, to my partner's return and to the comfort and familiarity of an evening together. I feel blessed.

Suffering and failing

We agreed, in our meetings and writings, that we would not evade what individuals saw as failures, or try to rationalise deep feelings of suffering, guilt, or disgust. This section concentrates on these aspects of our experience of sex.

It is not, however, easy to separate these out from the joys and pleasures of sexual experience. We all felt, from the start, the mixture of emotions and thoughts to which sexual feelings give rise or in which they find themselves expressed. This must be clear throughout this book. But nowhere more so than where we consider what exists beyond and in contrast to our happiness and sense of self-worth, and our sense of what is right, good, Godly, and wise.

It took the group a long time to reach the situation in which individuals could share the narratives in this section. Some of the things said here had not been said before, to anyone. We appreciate that some of the things said here may find a painful counterpart in your life, or in the life of someone you love.

Sometimes, to say 'I know just how you feel' is an evasion; and it is always some sort of nonsense. Nothing, however, brought us closer to others in the group than the things which are written here.

Fear breeds fear. I can't separate my own fear of being abandoned from that of my mother. I decided that I wasn't going to be as vulnerable as my mother. I wasn't going to sit around at home, sick with anxiety, wondering when, or if, he would come back. I decided that I was going to cope alone.

I was already well disposed towards independence at an early age: couple this with my determination not to be as vulnerable as my mother and it's not surprising that I failed to learn how to be dependent, or that it was safe to lean on someone sometimes.

My independence was forced, not chosen. It didn't evolve naturally from the dependence of childhood to the healthy interdependence of adulthood, and there was a resulting deformation. I became trapped by my independence, isolated in it. Outwardly strong, I was, inwardly, desperate to lean, to become a child again. I was longing to depend, but terrified to do so.

❖

My father was a kind man and I loved him dearly, but he lacked courage. I have such a sense of waste and tragedy. He sold out and failed to be true to himself.

In photographs of him as a young man he looks full of *joie de vivre*, with an energy that crackles and almost leaps off the paper. He looks straight out of the picture, arm round a friend, or sprawled on the summer grass, relaxed and full of fun.

Most of my memories are of a very different person: quiet, more self-contained, with the spirit gone, and symbolically his exuberant hair turned white and smooth where once there were waves.

I remember years of appalling conflict as he and my mother fought, with victory for my mother as the eventual outcome, though – in reality – they both lost. He somehow recognised that if the marriage was to continue he would have to toe the line. And he did. He buried his energy and extraversion, became a quiet, dutiful husband, concerned that she shouldn't get upset, and deferring to her on every issue and we followed suit. We were all in the business of keeping Mum sweet. She was the centre of everything. We all orbited around her.

❖

When I think of the word 'mother' what comes to my mind is stiffness, boundaries, distance, formality, FEAR. Over the years I have sought to go through the motions of being a good daughter but I have not given myself. What I have let her see is not the real me and – at some level – she knows it and it is her loss. We don't relate in a full human way: she hasn't a real daughter and I haven't a true mother.

❖

And never a child, because to relax meant the sky might fall and to dance and be playful was to invite disaster. God, did this make me feel weary. And now I feel angry about what I was denied: not only gentleness and love, but the opportunity to feel myself a child, to be playful and spontaneous, to be angry and sad.

I am aware as I write of enormous tension, of the importance of never putting a foot wrong. She was like a volcano ready to erupt without warning. She believed 'a bloody good hiding' would put right what was wrong in a child. How was it that I can remember being hit only twice? I was a cypher, not a real live flesh and blood child and, if I did overstep the mark, quickly quelled into submission by a basilisk glare.

❖

I have such a sense of the sins of the father (in this case the mother) being visited on the children. My mother's own experience was of being born into a world where she wasn't wanted, and this was at the root of a deep sense of the worthlessness that she had – no stake in the past – no claim on the future. And this guilt at existing at all had been reinforced relentlessly by the joyless circumstances of her childhood.

My mother remained loyal to my father, although we all tried to persuade her to leave him. It had not been a happy marriage, full of intimidation and dishonesty on his part and manipulation and secrecy on hers. She repeatedly enjoined us, 'Don't tell your father'. My sympathies always lay with my mother. She was trapped in a relationship, which to me offered her so little. Trapped by her marriage vows, by society's norms and, from my point of view, her fear of being on her own and a burden to her children.

Even as I sit in my study at home to try and write this piece I am aware that there is no way that I could begin to share any of it with my father who is staying with us at present. There is almost a complete breakdown of my communication with him so that to share anything of an intimate nature seems impossible. Yet he has recently taken to giving me the detail of the blood-stained sheets of his wedding night. I can hardly bear it and yet I mutely listen. I, who in my professional life am so assertive and even train others in the skills of clear, honest, direct communication, I, of course, did not have blood-stained sheets on my wedding night, as he well knows. To misuse the sharings of the intimate life of his then bewildered 18-year-old daughter is still unforgivable. It is part of the constraint I now feel about trying to share my thoughts and feelings about this most personal and private part of me: that what I write will be misunderstood and may be used against me and I will be impotent in my response.

❖

It has taken some years to dream this dream: I am in my bed, my childhood bed. My father is standing by my bed touching my genitals. At first I panic – 'Where's Mummy? Where's Mummy?' And then a scream of terror in my chest and throat tries to explode but can't get out – 'That's enough. That's enough.' It is a silent scream. I am desperate for someone to hear. But no one hears and I am sucked down into a deep, drugged sleep. Anaesthetised. Silenced.

It is my child voice that touches me: 'That's enough. That's enough.' I couldn't say 'Stop' or simply 'No'. I didn't say those words to an adult. I was taught to be polite to adults. 'That's enough' was the only way I knew to try to stop things happening. It was how I stopped my mother giving me too much spinach. 'That's enough, thank you.'

After this dream I am strangely relieved (it is about two weeks before the shock hits me). Now, for the moment, I am relieved feeling this dream to have offered the key with which I shall unlock part of my experience and throw light on some of the shadows. As a middle-aged woman I am now finally able to assert some boundaries and create a sense of safety for myself. It feels so good.

❖

My father and uncle look at my emergent breasts, laughing and saying, 'Aren't you getting busty!' Hot, silent embarrassment on my part.

My brother urgently corners me in the garden shed. He wants to fuck me.

I take tea up to my father who is resting in bed. I go into the room. He is sitting on the side of the bed with just his vest on. I can see – God, what can I see? Something large, red and repulsive. I put down the tea and back out of the room. Does he know what I saw? Did he mean me to see it?

❖

It still feels new and unfamiliar for me to say 'I was abused by my father.' I sense far-reaching shock-waves of these words. Such scandalous words thrown into the surface calm of what everyone conspired to believe was love and trust and respectability. Destroying the surface calm is an outrage. I am a monster for doing it, for having the nerve to expose what has, perhaps for generations, gone unspoken. As if I am the great betrayer. There are times when I fear I made it all up; times when I fear I didn't make it all up... and times when I fear there may be more to come.

❖

In my work I have had to listen to many men talking about their sexual fantasies and I have found them hard to take sometimes. But I don't think I could say they disgust me. My overwhelming feeling has usually been one of profound sadness at the bleakness of the relationships in the life of the man talking. And if you can start some sort of dialogue you usually find a depressed, lonely figure trapped in an expectation of sexual pleasure which is so masturbatory and turned in on itself, so lacking in the joy of mutuality that it is a caricature of all that we usually mean by love. It doesn't disgust me but it saddens and repels me.

❖

I see a woman waiting at a bus-stop: she is wearing a short black skirt, high-heels and fishnet tights.

I feel a sudden hollow longing for her, not just in my groin, but in my chest and abdomen, and in my thighs. But, even in my mind, she comes no nearer than she actually is: the longing I have for her is of that kind which comes with non-optional distance attached.

❖

I once went to a stag night, while I was a student. There were some films shown, the images of which have stayed with me and can come to mind unbidden. These are sensations I don't want to feel and images which I don't want to see. I suppose that evening of men students having drinks, watching films and strippers, was one which disgusts me in retrospect. I think my disgust is a mixture of the moral and the aesthetic, and perhaps these images come at a place where the bad and the ugly are impossible to tell apart.

❖

I used to be fascinated by newspaper reports of rape and would always be driven to read them. The more I talk to women I know about the reality of their experience of rape and abuse, the more this fascination has diminished. My partner suffered physical abuse in her marriage and both she and I are living with the consequences.

I am leaving my 9 a.m. class. It has been raining, the pavement shines as I dodge the dog-shit. I am wondering whether I've got time for a quick cup of coffee.

There are cars parked on either side of the narrow street. I am vaguely aware of a man standing on the pavement ahead of me.

I look up as I approach the man who seems to be waiting by the parked cars. He is looking straight at me and standing in my path. He is tall, perhaps 35, clean shaven and smart with a stylish hair cut. I notice a strange intense look about his forehead and eyes, his jaw is strained almost as if he's in pain and I'm aware of something moving in his hand. And then, suddenly, it's too late. Before thinking, I look down to see a small brown sack-like object swelling and flapping and bouncing in the air, in time to the rhythmic pumping of his hand.

Immediately I refocus my eyes on the road ahead, but the image of the half-inflated brown floppy bag won't go away. I am disgusted, nauseated. I am numb from the shock of having my eyes force-filled with this jerk's genitals. I am angry at having my morning invaded. I am angry with myself for not having realised, for being shocked, for not being cool and coming out with some witty deflating remark, for not having a sharp knitting needle handy.

He won. He had his orgasm and walked off, leaving me scared to look at all the other men now passing me on the street. I quickly turn round, half-fearing he may be following me. He has gone. But where has he gone?

❖

There is another memory I have from when I was very small. Someone had given me two feathered goosewings which I loved and played with in all kinds of ways: I was an angel, or a fairy. I was fascinated by the way I could open and spread the wings, with their beauty. One day I was sitting on the front doorstep, opening and closing one of the wings when I saw a line of maggots emerging from the wing. What had been so beautiful had become something revolting, that made my flesh creep.

I am sure all this is close to sexuality, but I find it hard to think of any particular sexual practices which in themselves arouse in me the same strength of feelings, though any kind of sexual act in which I was involved where the other was unwashed or reeked of smoke would disgust me.

For me disgust is very much to do with the senses and receiving messages that result in a physical response of me feeling sick. What makes me feel sick when I hear or read about it though it is beyond my experience? In the 1960s information was just emerging on the battered baby syndrome. I found it hard then and still find it hard that babies and children can be harmed and damaged to the point of death. The pictures that I have seen revolt me. I am absolutely clear that children have the right to be protected from such damaging and life-threatening experiences.

I am disgusted by the abuse of power in personal relationships. I tend to think that abusers are for the most part male and the abused are women and children. Why some people become abusers is an important question and the answers may give rise to a sense of disgust about a society that creates the conditions that lead to abuse. The same principles are in evidence where sexual relationships are concerned so that where harm or damage occurs either physically or emotionally, I have a sense of disgust and revulsion.

❖

Jealous; feeling nauseous. I cannot get to the end of this feeling. There is no deeper set feeling. All around you are in the field of jealousy. Any living thing to which you give your attention. Ownership: I need to own myself (through you). I need to own your brain. I am potential for jealousy. The feeling is like a prison.

❖

The tension which I experienced at this time stemmed from the phrase often repeated in church: 'Thy will, not mine...' From traditional Christianity I learned that God's Will was, by definition, not my own and (by implication) quite distinct from, even contrary to, my own will. During my adolescence, therefore, I was constrained not by specific prohibitions, but rather by a more all-pervasive restriction – one of having to search for an elusive Will which was not my own and which somehow emanated from an invisible world.

The effect of this constraint was to make illegitimate all my own needs, desires and wishes. Those things in life which attracted me (from career choice to clothes) could not possibly be 'right', by virtue of the fact that I was attracted to them. I was exerting my own will in wanting these things, therefore God could not possibly be present in them. All my choices were coloured by this dichotomy. I prayed and prayed for God to make 'His Will' plain. No answer. The result was that for many years I followed my own attractions and inclinations, feeling not so much guilty as continually dissatisfied.

Whatever enjoyment I did find as a result of my choices was always neutralised or edged with a tinge of regret, brought about by the knowledge that eventually when I did finally discover God's Will I would have to give up this enjoyment. There was a kind of pointlessness to everything, a disquieting, defeating awareness of another Will which would eventually intervene, which would inevitably negate my own emerging self.

❖

Ideals of self-control and sacrifice figured quite largely in my upbringing, although I didn't see it like that at the time. My inadequate attempts to articulate some sort of personal theology centre around the feeling that what I do is an important part of the destiny of mankind. If I can be an influence for good, in however small a way, then this is what God would want of me. If, on the other hand, I harm others by selfish desires, especially sexual desires, then I am not fulfilling God's purpose for me. What an impossibly high ideal! No wonder it leads to guilt and shame, when I know I have failed!

❖

I am sure that no woman ever wants to have an abortion. It is always the lesser of two evils. So I don't feel guilty about my decision to have an abortion but that doesn't mean that I don't think about it. I do quite often. I always assume I would have had a son, and I find myself thinking 'he would have been such and such an age now'. In a funny sort of way he is a member of the family, and has an existence. I used to wonder if the fact that I thought like this meant that I felt unresolved guilt and that I had in fact 'done wrong'. But I'm sure that the difficult decision we made was the right one for our family.

But I wish that at the time I had been able to confide in Friends. I wonder how many women in our meetings would feel they could go to an overseer and say, 'I'm pregnant and I don't feel I can go ahead with the pregnancy'. How many would then receive non-judgemental listening and help with sorting out why the thought of a child seems impossible and whether abortion is what the woman truly wants and is right for her and her family. Ideally I would see this a situation as the perfect case for a clearness committee – two or three Friends, acceptable to the woman, prepared to meet her and listen and ask the necessary hard questions. Because it will be a hard decision, whatever she decides to do, and she will need loving and prayerful support.

❖

I was once asked by a young man with end-stage AIDS whether he would be acceptable to God, since he was a homosexual. I shall never forget the look on his face. I could not answer the depth of despair with pious phrases about the inward light or that of God in everyone.

It required that I suffer alongside him. In October 1989, Meeting for Sufferings did not find clearness to make a public statement of our acceptance of homosexual people.* So would Barry – or I – be publicly acceptable to the God of the Quakers?

Writing proved impossible, but I hoped that I would have more inspiration after running a forenoon meeting on AIDS at Yearly Meeting. One member of my group fell into conversation with a friend who said, 'I thought about doing AIDS. But I realised that I don't need to do AIDS, I already know about it. You see AIDS is a disease of sinful people. So it won't be a problem for us.' Yearly Meeting has left me with more to think about, even if it did not directly provide the answers I was seeking.

In a recent book, the writer bewails the fact that, because of AIDS, the generations to come will not be able to enjoy uninhibited sexual encounters in the same way that the 'young people of the sixties' did. The unspoken assumption was that the sexual attitudes and behaviour before or since, being more restrictive, are or were therefore less fulfilling.

This made me very angry. I felt, 'OK, so for you the alleged sexual freedom of the sixties was how you were able to live and wanted to live, and now you are grieving its loss; but how do you know what those who are either older or younger than you, and who have quite different considerations to take into account, will be comfortable with?' It is too easy to make assumptions about other people's lives. It is also too easy to assume that living within a relatively restricted code of ethics is sure to lead to unhappiness.

My experiences as a parent and grandparent have, of course, included needing to work through the ways in which my children's attitude to their sexuality has differed from my own. I have also had many middle-aged or

* Meeting for Sufferings decided not to endorse a campaign to lower the age of consent for male homosexuals.

older members of the Society of Friends talking to me of their anguish about the decisions made by their adult children, so I know that I am not alone in having had to wrestle with this. There are so many feelings that surface at these times. 'Where have I gone wrong as a parent?' seems to be the one which brings in its train a load of guilt, when children go down paths that we have not foreseen, and would not have chosen for ourselves or them. 'What will the others think? Dare I tell anyone, especially within the Meeting? Is my children's behaviour a direct reflection on me?'

❖

Parental anxieties now seem to centre around the break-up of relationships, whether married or not, since this is the major difference in overt sexual behaviour in the past twenty-five years or so. Of our three children, one is married, one is living with a partner in a stable relationship (the third such partnership), and one is divorced. Statistically, this is a pretty average situation, although it would have been much less so a generation ago. Of our grandchildren, more than half are no longer living with their biological fathers. This is perhaps a little higher than the statistical average, but I know it is by no means an unusual experience for Quaker grandparents.

❖

I suppose in my own marriage I have been reacting to my parents' marriage. I have always been determined, particularly when the children were young, that we should do everything together as a family and that the children should be included in plans and decisions and that I would never be in a dependent position like my mother. I am sure that this reactionary approach, i.e. a determination not to repeat my parents' marriage, has created problems of its own. Nevertheless there is love and fun in my family that I did not experience.

❖

I can readily accept the thought of an adult couple deciding to part, providing that it is a well-considered, mutual decision. As a grandmother, and as someone who has had some experience of family conciliation work, what I still find difficult to come to terms with is the effect this has on any children concerned. I do not accept the argument that it can, other than in exceptional circumstances, be in the interests of children to lose a parent in this way. In the interests of the adults – quite possibly. In the interests of the children – seldom. Grandparents suffer too, and may need to mourn the losses that they can be experiencing at these times, but I have seldom seen any consideration of this increasingly common fact.

The common cry is, and possibly has always been, 'I am determined not to have the same kind of marriage that my parents had!' This is something else which makes me angry, if it is said in the kind of tone which implies that it is always wrong to stay together if the relationship is less than perfect. What relationship could ever be perfect, for goodness sake!

But when one says such things it can be taken wrongly to imply that what is meant is that there is only one 'right' pattern. All it implies is that it was right for me, given my background and the times that I have lived in.

❖

At this stage, while very much wanting a reconciliation, I was also impressed by the strength of my wife in not taking the easy way out. I had often prayed longingly that I might still yet be able to help fulfil her physically, emotionally, mentally and spiritually, but I had to begin to slay the dragon of possessiveness (another 'gift' of male conditioning) by letting go, admitting that I might not be the one and that the real gift of love would be to agree to a trial separation. Those who have gone through this type of trauma will recognise the symptoms of loss of weight and sleep and feelings of maximum insecurity. So we drifted into the rising divorce statistics, much to the sadness of our children and the concern and incredulity of others.

❖

It is ironic I suppose that my husband hurt me in a way that I am sure he did not fully realise. He fell in love with my brother's wife. I do not blame my husband or my sister-in-law. It happened out of common need and I spotted it too early for it to become a sexual relationship. This it seems to me is the paradox of sexuality. It can be wonderful and exalting and damaging and wounding at the same time. It is not something that just happens within a person; it is between people and it interconnects with everything.

❖

I remember, with the woman with whom I had my most successful sexual relationship, that I sometimes had a very hollow feeling after I had come. I remember, after this woman left her husband, I met him a couple of times. Now I can only think with fear of how I reacted all through that time, of lying, pretending, making up excuses for what I was doing, not thinking about the effect on him. Now, when I think of all that, I could cry, almost, with the deceit, the lack of basic decency involved. It's almost a feeling of self-disgust again, but this time along with the disgust, is a sort of sadness for the lost innocence.

❖

I don't think I shall ever lose the sense of failure that I have over the breakdown of my marriage. There are so many people I have let down: my former partner, my family, the Meeting, and above all my children. Whenever anything goes wrong in their lives – a relationship breaks up, one of them is depressed or has problems with work – my first reaction is to think that the loss of a parent at a critical age is partly to blame and therefore it is my fault.

And of course the person I have let down most of all is myself. The sense of shame and loss doesn't really go away. I made promises that I couldn't keep – to love until death us do part. When all my friends were celebrating their silver wedding anniversaries I couldn't help thinking that it should have been me – that if I hadn't made such a mess of my relationship I too could have been rejoicing in a partnership which had weathered the storms. I find it hard to forgive myself.

There are some things I have done that I cannot record. I cannot face them as they are unfictionalised, undramatised. I cannot say how I have hurt people, how I have deceived people. But my real fear is that I will be found out. I can say 'I have hurt and deceived people' in this abstract way, because that is a way of not saying that I have hurt and deceived people. It is a way of not saying it because it is the detail that accuses, and not the label 'hurtful' or 'deceitful'. It is a way of not saying it because it is me who says it, and not you.

Forgiveness is something that comes from other people. Accusation is something that comes from other people. People may accuse you and not forgive you.

My mind is not ready to be judged, because it has not heard the story of itself. It cannot hear that story unless you hear it too. To truly confess to someone, to confess the whole, and not to say what it is you have done wrong, but to let the story speak for itself, is hard. I want to tell my story with parentheses and explanations, footnotes and cross-references. But those parts of my story I need to tell cannot be told because it is not possible for me. I have a story I cannot tell, because I haven't the courage in my own mind to hear the story myself.

Paul Oestreicher once said that forgiveness is being able to remember without hate. I was very challenged in meeting last week when I was reminded that the move on from forgiveness is to remember with thankfulness. I find it very difficult to be in that position where my father is concerned. I am not in the position of being thankful that he is my father, but I have reached forgiveness and acceptance.

What is sin? In sexuality it is when relationships are not reciprocal, not acceptable and not synchronous. It is when the depths of myself are not included, when the process is not seen as the product, when forgiveness is not part of the equation and when insights are laid on another inappropriately.

I have tried to see if I came to a similar conclusion about sin if I came at it from the opposite side of the equation, i.e. when relationships are about intimidation, violence, exploitation, abuse and rape. I think the boundary is the same whether I come to it from a positive or from a negative standpoint.

reciprocity	intimidation
acceptance	violence
synchronicity	exploitation
depth (intimacy)	abuse, rape
journey	destination
forgiveness	hate
reticence	secrets or burdens

❖

Emerging into wholeness

Love is a process not a possession, and so this final section of our writings seeks to express something of the variety that the path of sexual experience has meant for us. Words that one of us once heard in a meeting for worship that perhaps summarise our experience as a group are imagination, integrity, compassion and wisdom. Maybe wholeness has to involve something of each of those attributes.

In our group process of emerging into wholeness we were amazed at the imagination and creativity of what was shared and that in turn helped each of us to contribute. The integration of pain and pleasure is part of this section. Suffering, conflict, misjudgement, betrayal are recognised as part of being human and the riskiness and adventure of love is mixed with steadfastness and ease of familiarity that long, deep relationships can experience. Compassion, for us, involved acceptance and affirmation of each other and a validation of our experiences as they slowly unfolded. Finally we found that wisdom came, sometimes unexpectedly, as we sought to find the way forward. Patiently listening to ourselves and each other helped us to be discerning and find the path.

One of the important ways of putting love – for ourselves and others – into action is to say 'No'. Boundaries are important but they are not fixed, just as creation and revelation are not yet complete – 'The Lord hath yet more light and truth to break forth from his word'. We need to respond with understanding to the truth that 'everything happens' rather than seeming to say 'anything goes'.

❖

To the extent that the Christian tradition has taught us mistrust of sexuality it has been wrong and oppressive. We are now emerging from the darkness of this ignorance and trying to learn how to live in full possession of our senses – not an easy process – confusion, trial and error are inevitable. We need patience with each other.

❖

Without the experience of pain, it is difficult to know how to bring healing to others. Yet many more people seem to me not broken open, but just plain broken – physically, emotionally, mentally and spiritually – by suffering. It is difficult to find meaning in that. Is suffering always for the benefit of the individual experiencing it? If there is any purpose in it at all, is it possible that people more often undergo suffering to induce growth and a change of attitude in the rest of us? 'And with his stripes we are healed' (Isaiah 53:5). AIDS is not God's punishment on those who have it; but God is challenging human society to show more love. I am well aware – and it is most humbling to realise it – that I have become a better human being, as well as a better doctor, from the suffering of my patients. Is this what the crucifixion – the central Western spiritual image – is about?

❖

Certain statements have informed or summarised my position over the years about being a woman such as:

> a woman's voice is important
> I have a voice and I will be heard
> there is nothing for the dumb
> women clean up other people's messes
> I want to be part of the equation

These are all very assertive statements but I hope they mean that I have moved on from the more manipulative way I used to be in relationships.

❖

How can someone who professes to be a pacifist, or at least one who tries to hold to the witness of the Quakers, find pleasure in giving someone else pain? How can one who would try to live in the light of the idea that there is that of God in all people find it a pleasure to humiliate another person?

If I say that these pleasures are sexual then it may make matters only worse.

Do you now have a picture of me? Am I the person with the police photofit look? Or the man in the dirty raincoat? Am I the fallen public figure, made fun of in the tabloids, or moralised over in the broadsheets? Am I the outwardly respectable business man or civil servant who leads a double life of shame and filth?

How dare you think so? What do you know about me, except that I have to cope with this; and that I am a human being? Who has the problem here, is it you or me? What is sticking in your throat – what is getting in the way of your accepting me, of coping with this part of me?

It is like an old friend to me, but one whom I had much better not have fallen in with. She is my misleader, and I don't like to bring her into your company – though she comes with me wherever I go, and I invite her, though often I shun her, and think I might be able to give her up, or draw away from her. But when a little time has passed, I meet her again, and greet her.

But how can I so misjudge you? Perhaps, far from thinking of me as a pervert, you are troubled, or concerned for me. Perhaps you are thinking that I will be saved, despite my desires to hurt and humiliate, by faith, or the grace of God. Perhaps you think that the love of God will enable me to fight this disease, help to put me back on the normal way, the right track. I don't know how to think of you if you think of me like this. Should I be grateful?

But perhaps your feelings are very different, and perhaps I have touched you in a way which troubles you for yourself. Do you have a passion which is an old friend, and which you are living with now, which you are ashamed of, and could not introduce to anyone else? Even those who love you, those who hate you, those who worship with you, do not know of this friend.

She diminishes you, because she is someone you don't quite like – of the wrong breeding, or views, or morals. But, perhaps she is why you worship, perhaps she reminds you, like the jester was said to remind the monarch, that you are only human, and that humanity has its unsafe districts, its places to avoid, that could do with cleaning up. Perhaps she is why you joined Friends, perhaps she is why you are gentle, why you try so hard to be kind, to care. Not in horrified reaction to her, but in the light of her existence.

I don't know you at all. I think we had better keep it like that. This must be a secret; I can only tell you this because we don't know each other.

❖

If I had not had a passionate affair in my late teens with a youth (scarcely old enough to be called a man) who was something of a sexual athlete, but whom I secretly scorned because he was not intelligent enough and not entirely honest, would I have been as content with a less sexually exciting partner (but who had all the other attributes which have proved to be of more lasting worth)? Maybe that was a useful learning experience for me, even though I must have hurt him when I dropped him immediately I went off to university and met lots of more interesting men. But later in life did I really need other men actively to show me that even though I was a wife and mother, I was still sexually attractive? – this I am not so sure of, and wonder if there could be any justification for my encouragement of such attentions. It seemed enjoyable fun at the time, but was it really necessary? As far as I know no real harm was done, but maybe that was more by luck than judgement. I was constrained by the moral climate of the time, together with the fact that contraception was not as efficient as it is now. I worry that the same behaviour today would be likely to be taken further and result in marriage break-up. I want to say 'it isn't worth it', but of course would only sound old-fashioned and out of touch.

I am on a 'high' at the present time with a feeling of constant thankfulness for what I have. After being married for forty years, we are reaping rich rewards in terms of our relationship. I find it difficult to write about, because the rewards are not in the terms which maybe could be understood by those that are younger. I learned very early on that you can't tell your children about the mistakes they should avoid, or the pitfalls they should be aware of – they have to learn things themselves by painful trial and error. So it is no good saying to those in the throes of a passionate love affair that the quieter affection of an older couple can be an even deeper experience. I know that this is just my experience, and it might not be the same for everyone. But this is all I can speak of with any certainty.

❖

Over the twenty-six years of my marriage I know that my perspective on what it means to be a woman has shifted, grown and developed. The fact that we are still married and have told each other that we would like to grow old together seems odd at times as our marriage has not been without its tensions, with more still to come, no doubt. We have tried to give each other the space to be who we can be. 'Spaces in our togetherness' probably sums it up. He would certainly claim that he has had to cope with more change on my part than I have on his. I would make an equal claim.

❖

I am now entering the menopause and so a new phase of my sexual life is about to begin. I cannot say I like it at present as my once so regular body and cycles are not so dependable now and I find the loss of control disturbing. I am regretting not having more children which is stupid at a rational level but very real nevertheless. It is all about change which brings opportunity as well as loss. The loss is about no longer being fertile.

❖

Whatever happened to the menopause?

I missed the menopause – or maybe it missed me. I was so busy living that it just passed me by.

True, my periods became irregular and I found myself in some awkward situations without protection; once or twice the bleeding was uncomfortably heavy. But that was it.

One day I woke up and thought, 'I don't believe I've had a period for six months. I must be through the menopause!'

I looked back and thought of one occasion when I might have had a hot flush, but then the room was warm and there was that sudden mutual attraction between a male colleague and myself as our eyes met across the table... I suppose at times I had been irritable, but no more than usual. So I'd acquired 'crone' status and felt a real surge of power.

Curious, that since the absence of that monthly reminder, I have become more aware of my body in many ways.

Interesting that, in the absence of an internal monthly clock, I have felt the need for an external one, and watch for the new moon and follow its progress minutely, aware, as never before, of its beauty and mystery.

❖

My advantage is that many of the more problematic stages of my life are now well behind me, and I can look back on them with a certain amount of tolerance. I do not expect to experience any further extra-marital emotional entanglements, and am content about that. After forty years of marriage, I expect to continue to live with my husband until death separates us, as the Quaker marriage vows say. I have no regrets about this, and do not feel I have missed out on anything by having only had one permanent relationship in my adult life. Quite the contrary, I have done too much work with couples who have entered into a succession of semi-permanent relationships, sometimes to the lasting sorrow of their children, to be envious of those who have appeared to have had a more adventurous sexual life.

Before I became a Quaker I struggled for many years with the question as to whether or not I had the vocation to become a nun. Strangely now to me in retrospect, the problem was not that I had worries about a life of celibacy; it was more to do with the nature of the call and the vow of unquestioning obedience. Embracing celibacy was something I was prepared, possibly eager to do.

I was reminded of that long ago era in my life when I recently worked alongside a nun who had spent all her working life in Africa. Her open attitude to life and loving acceptance of her fellow workers showed clearly that a celibate life joyfully entered into in the pursuit of a greater good than sexual fulfilment is not a deprivation or a perversion. It can enrich many lives. But outside the support of a community it can be hard to maintain in the face of the relentless pressures of our society.

❖

While I have thoroughly enjoyed and participated in the role of Dad, and I think as a couple we complemented each other well as parents, it was frustrating to have to put so much energy into career building (in order to provide for the family) when the children were so young. This is compensated by greater energy being available, but the contradiction remains.

We can all learn grace from our mistakes: some of us have to learn as adults how to build lasting and loving relationships. In the past I had a long relationship with another man which in the end became mutually abusive and very destructive. For some years now I have been favoured to have a close and loving gay relationship: our life together is an abundant means of expression of Christ's love. I have seen and experienced the best and worst that long-term relationships have to offer.

Many lesbian and gay people are parents; but it has not been given to either of us to have children of our own. This is a sadness to my lover but a relief to me. In common with many other people, of all sexual orientations or of none, we are released from the demands of rearing children. This gives us the time needed to nurture other vital things, including our Meeting and the wider Society of Friends. Apart from children, all the other blessings that are described as the purpose of marriage we have abundantly in our relationship.

The fact that I use the sacred word marriage in this context will distress many Friends. Is this an example of the letter that killeth (2 Corinthians 3:6)? I can think of no other word which comes close to describing the many aspects of our relationship adequately. My hope is that those who object will be given the grace to try to understand the spirit at the heart of another person's life and experience.

We have a Local Government Act in Britain. Section 28 says that Local Authorities must not 'promote homosexuality as a pretend family relationship'. This futile law is deeply and gratuitously offensive. We do not have a pretend family relationship, we have a real family relationship. Jesus reminds us that we know a good tree by its fruits

(Matthew 7:16-20). Look beyond prejudice and see how we love each other. See what our love's fruits are in our lives.

❖

The body of the Society of Friends certainly has AIDS already. Most Quakers are more tolerant and affirmative of gay people than other Christian groups. There are exceptions, though 'Why do you have to talk about it?' is more common than overtly expressed hostility, which does also exist amongst us. However one feels about homosexuality, the Society has been entrusted with the pastoral care of many gay people and the nurture of their spiritual talents. These include members, attenders and employees of the Society who have HIV or AIDS. AIDS does not only affect those infected. Quakers have friends, lovers, sons or daughters with the disease – or who fear they might have it. Many Quakers work with people who have AIDS, and grow to love them. It is emotionally gruelling to suffer multiple bereavement: that is an experience which AIDS workers – indeed all health care workers – share with many gay men nowadays.

❖

Another way of looking at the separation and divorce with its pain and sadness is that perhaps my wife and I were fulfilling important life lessons for each other, opening new possibilities and raising self-awareness by identifying each other's strengths, weaknesses, priorities and failures.

❖

Forty years of marriage has had joy and has had pain. The births of the children were happy times, but of course were also times of crisis, especially as we were extremely poor in those days. Our children still remember the day I am reputed to have thrown the cornflake packet at Dad – but they don't know that it was at a time when our sex life was not going well. We were still, after some years of marriage, not able to agree entirely on what was permissible sexually and what was definitely not on. I know from the work I have done, especially in marriage counselling, that every couple behaves differently in bed and has different expectations – there is no right and wrong, only what is mutually acceptable and not positively harmful. It's all very well knowing this in theory, but it took us a long time to work that out in practice – if we ever did. I don't know whether all couples have to work out compromises in their sexual lives, but we certainly had to.

We have both had times when we were attracted to others. As far as I was concerned, I enjoyed these times, did not tell my husband about them, never took them very seriously, and was quite happy when they faded out. It was only later that I was a little worried about having led someone on when I had no intention of allowing it to become permanent. I can remember one man getting to the point of asking me whether I would leave my husband, and I was deeply shocked that he would think such a thing. Another man, who was also married with young children, carried on a clandestine correspondence with me for a year or so, and we sometimes met secretly – but it was all very much on the 'Brief Encounter' lines, with the best thing about it being the romantic idea that it could never be more than an occasional walk in a park. I couldn't possibly have actually married either of these men. They wouldn't have suited me as husbands – and I had a perfectly adequate husband anyway, who was the father of our three children. It is of course quite probable that I only allowed myself to act on any attraction to another man when I knew it was 'safe'. Even recently I realise that, in a Meeting which was very loving, and where we all tended to kiss and hug each other whenever we met, I avoided kissing one fairly elderly male Friend because I felt a strong affinity with him.

My husband has also, to my knowledge, had a few times when he has been attracted to another woman. I have felt jealousy and hurt, especially the last time when I suppose I was becoming more vulnerable because of being older and less physically attractive. I would have liked to be able to take these situations more calmly because, apart from hurting my pride, I don't think he has seriously endangered our marriage any more than I have. I have been surprised how strongly I have felt, and at how feelings can take you unawares, especially in matters like this, however laid back one tries to be. I have often wondered whether, if we had been of a younger generation, we would have assumed falling in love with someone else meant the end of the marriage.

Now we are senior citizens. We haven't stopped having sexual feelings, or giving expression to these although the urgency and intensity of feelings are less. Not to put too fine a point on it, we would neither of us be capable of the same performance as when we were young. I can accept this, and it doesn't cause me any concern, although I know that men are alleged to feel badly when their sexual powers wane.

My appetite for marriage at present is greatly diminished. Inner changes of development as well as outer social changes are so rapid that to speak in terms of commitments for life seems inappropriate. To have love and caring for the moment is sufficient in itself – the future can take care of itself. This is what we agree as partners – for the present we can do no more. That is why we exchanged our pledge 'to be close and valued companions and partners for as long as we both shall grow in our togetherness; for as long as we both share our integrity and creative purpose. We ask that this our sacrament of unconditional giving and receiving to help fulfil our life's purpose, be a living witness of love to those whose lives we touch and be sanctified by the divine.'

As we get older, there is the knowledge that one day one of us is going to be left alone. I know that we both recognise the importance of enjoying the time we have together. Today has been a good day. It was warm for an autumn day. We had a gentle walk in a country park overlooking the sea and watched the seabirds and the passing shipping. We had tea sitting outside a little cafe at the top of the cliffs, and then drove slowly home. These kinds of experiences – the little things in life – are the moments which for me are spiritually the most telling. We have not been in the habit of having silence before meals until quite recently, but we always do now when we are on our own, because we are so grateful for the accumulation of small blessings which we have. We still irritate each other at times. We still argue about things like map-reading and our relative driving skills, but we still have our own private word for the special cuddle we have in bed before we go to sleep each night.

❖

The Gulf War has felt as if it is inside of me and I have felt I was Saddam Hussein. Terrible things leap out of the newspaper and engage and threaten to overwhelm me: the ordeal of the Birmingham Six, slopping out in prison, one in seven women raped in marriage, Clause 28. How can such things happen? I feel so angry and powerless at what seems such injustice and complacency. And the tiniest thing seems to have the power to plunge me into gloom and sadness. But then, there are moments of great beauty and perhaps 'wholeness'. Yesterday afternoon I was lying on the sofa reading, with the sun streaming through the window and with a background of Mozart clarinet music. Suddenly I was overwhelmed with the incredible beauty of it all – the pot of daffodils, the grain on the oak table and the blue, blue sky beyond. Everything I looked at was suffused with an amazing clarity and immediacy. I felt part of the blue Chinese dragon that was the cushion beside me and it was part of me, and even the barbed wire on the fence through the window was imbued with a strange grotesque beauty.

❖

I read Paul Tillich's *Shaking of the foundations* at university and found it really exciting and so different from the evangelical literature that I was used to reading. The phrase which I have remembered ever since was about 'accepting the fact that you are accepted'. That is a very important theological statement for me and has stayed with me and stood me in good stead in times of doubt. I might feel guilty, ashamed or depressed, but that sense of acceptability is real. 'I'm OK, you're OK' is another way of putting it... If I have a visual image of God it is of a presence covering my back so that I can stand with confidence facing whatever I have to face, knowing that I am completely accepted and supported. Of course I cannot see God from this position: I just trust that presence to be where I need it, covering where I am vulnerable and letting me stand tall.

Since we started our discussions, I have been living with one central question which has come up in different forms again and again and which has also been expressed by others in the group: 'Is love trustworthy?' 'How do I know that my love won't be betrayed or abused?' 'What about the inevitability of loss/death?' 'Can I give myself to the experience of desire which at once opens me fully to the Spirit, yet also seems to threaten the stability and security of my world?' 'How can I allow the experience of passion into my life, with the heightened illumination this brings, when it also seems to be accompanied by deep 'unsettlement', anguish, the pain of conflicting loyalties and jealousy, etc.?' It is clear to me, intellectually and theologically, that the body and the spirit are not opposed to each other, but my experience has taught me that the senses can lead to too much vulnerability, chaos and danger.

What I see emerging here are not fundamentally moral or ethical questions, but spiritual ones about faith and doubt. All great spiritual teachers have shown by the example of their lives that our spiritual quest is one which leads to the fullest possible surrender of our selves and souls to God, that the sole purpose of life is to learn to abandon ourselves increasingly to divine love and providence. What happens, then, if most of our experience has taught us to be suspicious of love and of passion; if our only experience of what we believed was 'love' has been negative?

I fall in love. I am suddenly as vulnerable as a child. The object of my love can be taken away from me, and I fear that I shall fall into a black hole of non-being. I struggle to secure some assurance, some proof that I am 'really loved'. My society teaches me that sex is the expression of love par excellence. Sex will prove to me that I am loved. Yet I cannot escape the subconscious knowledge that sex doesn't provide this proof, so my fear is, in fact, deepened.

Sex is supposed to be the way in which I experience my most profound moments of intimacy and self-transcendence. Yet, more often, I have used it (unconsciously) to try to provide myself with guarantees of security. Sex therefore becomes a way in which I short-circuit the very experience I seek – intimacy. Sex becomes a defence mechanism. Through sex I reinforce my ego boundaries rather than transcend them.

It's not really surprising, then, that I have experienced the body as dangerous. Sex has brought me closest to the knowledge of the existence of the black hole of emptiness. I have had to learn that there are no shortcuts to attaining the knowledge that I am loved and that I can be safe in love. If I can't discover it within and for myself, I shall never be able to believe that I am truly loved by another person. And, paradoxically, if I don't experience myself as being loved by others (however much I may doubt it), I cannot find love in myself. Here I think I am brought very close to the mystery of love's work, and finally to the act of grace which alone can reveal love's trustworthiness to us.

I am trying to liberate myself from the need to possess love. I am trying simply to enjoy the blessing of love and to trust the process of love as it unfolds in my life, trying to stop looking for guarantees and happy-ever-after endings. This isn't as easy as it sounds.

I know I've come a long way. I've learnt to distinguish between my passion which comes from God, and my compulsive, addictive behaviour which comes from a big black hole of need within me. I've learnt about boundaries and how to take care of myself. I've learnt to look for relationships in which the rewards are equal to my investment. I'm learning to release my fear and to trust that I can be guided by my feelings.

None of this is what I expected. Sex and relationships haven't turned out to be what I was led to believe they would be. None of the messages I received from family, school or church spoke to the condition in which I subsequently found myself. Consequently I feel I am emerging from a haze, from an exile of incomprehension. I dared to struggle for clarity, dared to believe in the Truth which is revealed through my own experience. It has been an adventure. My faith has deepened, grace has often intervened and I am thankful for it all.

❖

This is a list of things that, on reflection, I would have liked/wanted/needed from a religious institution about my emerging sexuality, although I might not have been able to articulate it at the time. While I am relating this particularly to religious institutions I think it is equally applicable to any group that pronounces on sexuality such as families, schools and communities.

I needed an institution that would:

inform me appropriately about my sexuality **not** keep me in ignorance about my sexuality

encourage my sexual development **not** prohibit and so inhibit my sexual development

help me to feel good about my sexuality **not** make me feel bad/sinful about my sexuality

protect me and keep me safe **not** stifle me or imprison me or expose me to damage and abuse

allow me/enable me to be open about my sexuality **not** repress me and demand conformity to unrealistic standards

forgive my mistakes **not** condemn my wrongdoings

help me to be mutually considerate of my needs and those of my sexual partner, whether lifelong or brief **not** demand either passive submission or domination in a relationship

be realistic and truthful **not** set impossibly high standards, be hypocritical or give mixed messages

love me and accept me, whatever orientation my sexuality takes **not** only promote one excluding relationship, *ie* heterosexuality within marriage

encourage me to meet my sexual needs in relationships that are healthy, consenting, reciprocal and careful of outcomes **not** to use relationships, espeçially marriage, to assuage my passion and legitimise non-consenting outcomes

validate me as a sexual person that sees my sexuality as an integral part of me **not** continually separate my sexuality from the whole of me (body, mind, spirit split) and then seek to subjugate my passion

respect privacy **not** lead to deceitful secrecy

promote enjoyment and fun **not** guilt and regret

lead me to discover, harming others as little as possible in the process, the boundaries of appropriate sexual behaviour **not** prescribe, without allowing experimentation, what is permissible

deal with me in an age-appropriate way **not** in a patriarchal paternalistic way, regardless of my age

encourage shared responsibility in relationships **not** seek to apportion blame and punishment

help me to be articulate about my sexual needs **not** coy, devious or deceitful

I realise as I have written this list that I still need all these things. Not receiving them has led to massive amounts of guilt, deceit and hard work to reach a place of acceptance about my sexuality.

TOGETHER IN FRIENDSHIP

The idea of the Quaker meeting as a place of friendship is a vital one if needs are to be met and if growth is to be a matter of course and we can live up to our name as the Religious Society of Friends.

It is within the context of this place of friendship – 'where two or three are gathered together', trusting in the presence of the Spirit – that we believe our ethical decision-making must happen. Any sexual ethic which is to have integrity for us and which is to be consistent with the Quaker and Christian tradition, must be one which arises from the gathered community; one which arises from a process of working together in love.

In order for this to happen, our meetings need to be more than just places for Sunday morning worship. They need to become communities in which our love and care for each other are a reflection of the love and unity we sense in our relationship with God. In George Fox's words:

> Therefore keep your meetings, and dwell in the power of truth, and know it in one another, and be one in the light, that you may be kept in peace and love in the power of God, that you may know the mystery of the gospel: and all that ever you do, do in love; do nothing in strife, but in love, that edifies the body of Christ, which is the church.*

We believe that clarity about what is good and what is right comes as a result of corporate seeking and discernment. We learn about discernment together as we deepen in our commitment to be seekers with one another after the truth. Janice Raymond says that

> the habit of discernment teaches us to be loyal to ourselves, to have faith in our own insights, and to claim these as the power of scrutiny in our interactions with others. Discernment is not foolproof, nor can it guarantee that friendship lasts for ever. What it provides is insight, even insight into our own mistakes.†

* George Fox, *A collection of many select and Christian epistles...*, vols 7 and 8 of *The works of George Fox*, Gould and Hopper, 1831, vol 8, p 42.

† Janice Raymond, *A passion for friends*, The Women's Press, 1986.

Truth about what is good or right does not come to us as a disembodied proposition, unmediated by human minds and hearts. Truth is fundamentally relational and personal in nature. If we take to heart this understanding of the nature of reality and of truth, it has profound implications for the ways in which we live our lives and search for ethical and moral clarity. It demands that we be willing to create a space in which relationships can flourish and in which the accompanying tension, risk-taking and vulnerability may be sustained and upheld. It also demands that the methods and structures we choose to help us create this space be consistent with our commitment to the relational and personal nature of the truth we seek together.

We hope that the process we have used in writing this book might offer Friends an example of how such a space may be brought about. Although this process is challenging, there can be safe places where we can meet each other, acknowledging our human frailty and withholding judgement but accepting and coming at last to understand our common experience of that of God within each one of us.

Structures will of course differ from place to place and time to time. It is for each person to decide the forms and structures which would best facilitate a process of exploration for them. For us, creative listening has been a vital tool which we commend to Meetings. This is a practice which aims at removing the stresses sometimes found in group discussion where the strongly expressed views of certain people may deter others less sure of themselves from voicing their experience. They may fear being rebuffed or simply feel inadequate at expressing themselves or feel, wrongly, that they have no contribution of value to make. Creative listening is concerned to give value to everybody's contribution. It concentrates on the group's attempt to listen to each other at a deep level through foregoing the chance to comment on, reply to, or dissent from anything that anyone else says. What is said within the group remains confidential: nothing should be revealed to anyone outside the group, not even to a spouse or partner, without the consent of the person involved. In this way a place of trust is provided and assured for everybody. We often have false preconceptions about other people because we know too little about where their experience comes from or what leads them to speak and act as they do. Creative listening can help us in overcoming these preconceptions.

The practice is straightforward. The group adopts a simple contract. Each person speaks in turn without interruption, either using a prearranged sequence such as going around in a circle or as the spirit moves. It is acceptable for someone who does not feel able to speak to indicate that fact and remain silent. It may be helpful to set an approximate time limit on the length of each person's contribution, so that each has a proper opportunity to be heard. What is said should be spoken from personal experience and not be a statement of theoretical ideas. For some people this is difficult to achieve. There should be no evaluative comment on what anyone has said. These conditions can lead to a radically changed atmosphere of understanding and acceptance, since there is no pressure in the group to mould the other participants' views. The facilitator of such a group should be aware that sometimes powerful emotions and experiences may be released and that participants need to be ready to share each other's joys and to support each other in anxiety or distress. One of us has written:

> Total personal openness with others is not necessary or advisable, though it is helpful to know that others have similar experiences to me, as then I feel less isolated. But openness to myself is perhaps more important. If I am honest with myself about my own life story, it should help me to be more compassionate with others, shouldn't it? 'He that is without sin ... let him first cast a stone'.

Friendship is about the possibility of finding our true selves and all that we can be for ourselves and others. It involves loving care for ourselves and others. That loving care includes the need to be courageous and honest about our thoughts and feelings and to be able to recognise and express them, when appropriate, in a way that is tender and strong at the same time. It is also about receiving other people's thoughts and feelings in the same spirit of possibility for growth.

❖

Further guidance about creative listening groups can be found in *Meeting needs: a handbook for Quaker groups and meetings.**

* *Meeting needs: a handbook for Quaker groups and meetings*, edited by Stuart Randall for the Quaker Networks Project, Quaker Home Service, 1992.

We suggest the following queries as a help to individuals and meetings wanting to enter more deeply into the challenge of friendship and discernment:

- In what ways have my Christian or Quaker traditions affected me sexually?
- What are the costs and risks of talking openly with others about my sexuality?
- Do I cherish my sexuality as a God-given gift and try to integrate it with the rest of my being?
- Do I embrace my sexual relationships as an opportunity to meet that of God in my partner? Do I recognise that these opportunities for close communion can also, if mishandled, lead to rejection and alienation?
- Where do I draw the line on what is or is not permissible sexual behaviour for myself?
- What role does sexual fantasy play in my life?
- To what extent can I commit myself to a lifetime with another person?
- What is my attitude to other people's sexual practices which are different from my own?
- How do I respond to the changing perception of marriage in society today?
- Can love involving sexual relations be maintained with more than one person at the same time?
- What support or guidance can we give when sexual feelings change in a continuing relationship?